My Thoughts Exactly

My Thoughts Exactly

LILY ALLEN

BLINK
bringing you closer

Published by Blink Publishing
2.25, The Plaza,
535 King's Road,
Chelsea Harbour,
London, SW10 0SZ

www.blinkpublishing.co.uk

facebook.com/blinkpublishing
twitter.com/blinkpublishing

Hardback – 978-1-911-600-89-3
Trade paperback – 978-1-911-600-90-9
Ebook – 978-1-911-600-92-3

A CIP catalogue of this book is available from the British Library.

Typeset by Envy Design
Endpaper design © Steve Leard
Printed and bound in Great Britain by Clays Ltd, Elcograf S.p.A.

1 3 5 7 9 10 8 6 4 2

Blink Publishing is an imprint of Bonnier Books UK
www.bonnierbooks.co.uk

George, Ethel & Marnie

CONTENTS

INTRODUCTION

First, a few facts. They're important, because this isn't a normal memoir where you find everything out in the order that it happened. I'm too young to write my life story and I've got no interest in remembering event after event after event. This is how much of this book would read if I did that:

Got up. Hair. Make-up. Clothes. Studio / shoot / performance. Emails. Went out / performed / worked / partied. Got on aeroplane / tour bus / in car. Did it all again, then again. And again. Cycle interrupted by birthing and looking after children – before doing it all again.

To a degree.

It's the degree I'm interested in: the things in my life that changed events, upended things, upset the cart. Sometimes, these were external events I had no control over: my son, George, was born three months prematurely, but had already died inside me; I was stalked for seven years and felt my life threatened by someone with a severe mental illness, then witnessed his trial – I've been through episodes of mental ill-health myself, so I felt for him despite what he did to me, as it's no fucking picnic; I've been sexually harassed as an adult by someone in a position of power and whom I trusted; and I was taken advantage of sexually as a young teenager by men who should have known better. Turns out, it's an all-too-common experience. (Me too.)

Sometimes it was me, myself, who wreaked havoc on my own life, as you'll see. (Self-destructive.)

By contrast, some of the things that have changed my life have been more joyous than I could ever have imagined. I have two daughters, Ethel and Marnie. I've had success in a career known for its ruthlessness, and which thrives by rejecting most of its applicants, eschews internships and dispenses with training. But I've found a path through it. I've been showered with kindness and generosity. I've been spoilt. I've been invited everywhere, made to feel welcome, and I've often been applauded – sometimes by tens of thousands of people. I've played the Pyramid Stage at the Glastonbury Festival, not once but three times. (Get me.)

But the same industry that rewarded me has also been punitive. This is not a complaint (not here, anyway), but a fact. I'll explain more as we go along. I've been bullied and pilloried and humiliated, in public, by the press. The tabloids, as we all know well, especially after the Leveson Inquiry, operate on a venal, pernicious, dishonest and abusive basis. Young people, women especially, are easy fodder for them to bully, especially when we are new to fame and success, and a bit puffed up with the novelty of it all, while still being naïve and easily bruised, quick to take offence and easy to bait. I've taken the bait sometimes. I've learned some difficult lessons, and made a load of mistakes, but I've also been spied on and followed and had my words twisted into lies, and that has been paralysing and isolating.

I've made friends through work and lost them. But I've also got friends I've had since I was a small child. That is a blessing. In fact, mostly I've been surrounded by love, even when I've felt profoundly unlovable. We all live with shadows. Mine have been magnified somewhat because I'm in the public eye, but I don't claim them to be darker than anyone else's – it's just that I can only talk about my own, and at times they've felt pitch-black. Sometimes, I made them darker than they needed to be, but it can be hard to let the light in when you're troubled. I've been troubled.

This is the story of all those times, and my thoughts about them. It's not a straight memoir. It's not even a straight story. Is any?

It is *my* story. It's entirely true to me – but I don't claim it to be the only truth. For example, my brother will have his own version of events, even though we were born sixteen months apart and grew up next to each other. So will my ex-husband, even though we were together for six years, much of that time happily, and had three children together, and had to bury one. We bring up our daughters together, still.

So, this is me. I am Lily Allen. I was born in 1985. I'm a songwriter and a singer, a mother, daughter, sister, home-maker. I was once a wife. I'm someone's girlfriend. That someone is called Dan, and he's a musician, too. I'm an activist – socially and politically. I'm a tweeter. I'm a Labour voter. I'm a writer. I've been a success and a failure. I'm unqualified and mostly self-taught. I didn't go to university, didn't do A-levels, didn't sit a single GCSE.

I didn't grow up in a particularly musical household, but performance was always around me; the media world was never a special or glamorous beacon, but my norm. My mum, Alison Owen, is a film producer. My dad, Keith Allen, is an actor, comedian and documentary maker. My step-dad for a time was the comedian, Harry Enfield. I've got an older half-sister called Sarah; a younger brother, Alfie; and a much younger half-sister called Teddie. (I have other half-siblings, too, but I don't know them or even know how many there might be – not a straight story.) My first boyfriend was Lester. My best friend is Seb, and we now work together, too. He's a music producer. The man I married is called Sam Cooper, and he has a building company. We separated in the autumn of 2015.

I grew up going to Glastonbury and the Groucho Club. My dad was part of the Britpop scene, getting publicly loaded with his friends Damien Hirst, Alex James and others. Drugs and alcohol have been part of my white noise – always around me – for as long as I can remember. I have used both, sometimes to excess, and although I've been to NA and AA meetings and have had sober periods of my life, I am not a recovering alcoholic or drug addict. I do, however, suffer with depression. (Not a straight story.)

I did go to various private schools, as well as state ones,

but didn't stay at any of them for very long, so I'm not a product of any one particular system or institution. I started singing as a child at school, but discovered music as a young teenager and kept it close to me from then on. I read. I keep notebooks. I've got a good eye. I collect textiles, love colour, and decorating or doing up a house doesn't faze me at all. I exercise but I'm not a natural athlete. I'm a swimmer. I'm strong. I can be tough. I've been broken. I'm opinionated. I'm a people-pleaser. I'm a narcissist. I'm co-dependent. I don't always like being alone, though equally there are times when I can't bear company. I'm spoilt. I'm needy. I can be a hypocrite. I contradict myself. I can be cold.

But I can also see sense. I can connect the dots. I try to do good. I want to do good. I'm impassioned. I'm observant and I notice things. I have a photographic memory. I remember names, places, things, although there are whole periods of my life that are hazy and washed out – the lights are out. I cook, not all the time, but often. I'm a trained florist. I drive well and have an excellent sense of direction. I'm financially independent and make my own money, sometimes quite a lot of it, but I also run up debt. I made my own way in my career. You have to. Even if you get a leg up, there's no other way to do it.

I find a lot of things funny, and I laugh a lot, sometimes even when things aren't that funny. Sometimes it's like a tic. Laugh, Lily, laugh, and it'll make things easier, lighter, more absurd. Right? Not always. Often not.

Like most women I know, I juggle a lot – work, children, family, money, running a household, steering my own ship.

But I haven't always managed. I've fucked up a good deal. I can be a fuck-up. You'll see.

I tell the truth. I am writing this because writing is what I do. It's both my living and the way I live, the way I make sense of things, the way I try to learn my lessons. I am writing this so that if I died today, my daughters can learn from my mistakes, and so that whatever information they may stumble on about me (I imagine them as adolescents googling my name), there will be a version in black and white that will not alter in the retelling. Fuck, I'm writing this so that *I* can learn from my mistakes.

I am writing this to tell my story because telling stories is important, especially if you are a woman. When women share their stories, loudly and clearly and honestly, things begin to change – for the better. This is my story.

THE OUTSIDER

Growing up, I felt like the outsider in my family. My early years feel hazy and out of focus, as if I didn't have edges or definition. It's unattractive to complain too much about your childhood, and playing the victim – even if you genuinely feel like one – isn't appropriate or constructive in a story like mine. It also isn't necessarily the truth. It's *a* truth. That doesn't make the story any less valid, but it's worth noting. There are so many truths and versions of any story, but the ones from childhood are especially shape-shifting because that's when you should be experiencing everything in the moment most particularly. My truth is that I didn't feel nurtured as a child. I felt lost and invisible and often ignored. That lack of care, or what I take to be a lack, has informed much of my behaviour as an adolescent and an adult.

My mum became pregnant with my sister Sarah when

she was eighteen. She wasn't married. She gave birth alone because the night she went into labour, Sarah's dad was at a Clash concert in Brighton, and her own mum, a staunch Catholic, didn't accompany her to the hospital because she disapproved of the pregnancy. Mum had no one to hold her hand that night. I didn't know that until later on in my life, but it explains a lot to me about my mum and my sister and their extraordinarily tight bond. It must have started that night when they went through that experience, just the two of them. They survived together.

I felt outside their circle. I felt like I had to survive on my own, and as if I was low down on my parents' list of priorities: below their careers, and less important than Sarah or my baby brother, who arrived sixteen months after I was born. However much Alfie and I were together – and we were always bundled up together and treated like peas in a pod – I was also quite an independent little thing, more of a loner than my siblings.

I didn't find a slot outside our family unit, either. Alfie was passionate about football, for instance, but, by contrast, I wasn't into anything in particular; not gymnastics or ponies or dolls or climbing trees or make-up or being a tomboy.

I know I was loved as a child, but I didn't *feel* that love very much. My parents were away a lot, absent because of work (Mum) or play (Dad). They were young when we burst into their lives, and they were busy forming themselves while we were growing up. They both came from provincial, working-class families, and they both made it to London and into media careers. They reinvented themselves away from their families and their roots, and that's hard to do. It takes work and energy and focus.

It meant there wasn't too much time left over for us kids, so their attitude towards us was along the lines of, 'The kids'll be OK. Let's let them get on with it.' As kids, we were left alone a lot. Encouraging us to find hobbies or after-school activities was too much of a commitment and reliant on a routine they had no interest in. (I went to my first weekend activity after Mum got together with Harry, and they signed me up for junior cordon bleu cookery classes on Saturday mornings. I loved it.)

Instead, I read a lot and loved listening to audio books. I watched a lot of TV. The Australian soaps, *Neighbours* and *Home and Away*, on at teatime each day, were part of my daily routine. In the morning, before school, I watched breakfast TV. I felt like Gaby Roslin was my TV mum. She looked a bit like my real mum and seemed in control of whatever situation she found herself in. I liked that about her. Even back then I knew that she wasn't prepared to suffer humiliation, at least not because she was a woman who was usually in a sea of lads. Most of all I liked that she was always there. I switched on the TV and there she was, always available, never busy or distracted.

We weren't a family that did things together. My parents didn't seem to be a couple that did things together, either. Certainly, I didn't witness them having any kind of loving relationship. I believe my mum fell totally in love with my dad when they met and got together, and I know she felt bereft and let down by him when he walked out on us. But even when they were together, I don't remember good times. Maybe I was too young. Maybe they didn't happen all that often.

I didn't give all this much thought until recently. When I was young, all my friends' parents were divorced. It was just the way things were. No big deal. But it is a big deal, I now realise.

The first time my boyfriend Dan's son came to stay with us, not too long ago, he was three years old. We spent the weekend together, me and Dan, his boy, and my girls, hanging out as a family. After the weekend, Dan told me about a conversation he'd had with his ex. He told me how he had reassured her, 'Lily and I weren't kissing and cuddling or holding hands in front of the kids.' And she'd replied, 'I don't have a problem with you showing affection to Lily in front of the kids. In fact, it's important for them to see how adults behave with each other when they are in love.'

When Dan relayed this conversation to me I thought, *How astute this person is*. I couldn't stop thinking about what she had said. Then it hit me. *Oh my God*, I thought. *I never saw that when I was young*. As a child, I didn't witness any adults in a loving relationship or showing each other affection.

Thinking about this affected me deeply. It felt like I'd found a piece of the puzzle as to why I've felt like a vessel (OK on the surface, empty inside) for so long. Because if you say to me, *Lily, how did you feel growing up? Did you feel happy or content or loved, did you bumble along in the moment without too many cares?* – which is how I imagine children should, if possible, grow up – then my answer is this: as a child (and often as an adult), I felt like a beating heart and pile of skin, but nothing more: nothing substantial or filled up or whole.

MOTHERS

My mum is Alison. She was brought up in a religious family in Portsmouth, but quickly chose to worship at the altars of socialism and punk rather than Catholicism. She is smart and bright, funny and beautiful. Sometimes, people think they've got the measure of her, but they haven't. She's blonde and sexy, with big boobs, and she's all about her brain. She's a big brain inside a funny little lady. She knew from the get-go that she wanted a career, and that she wanted it in film, and yet even though she was hugely ambitious, she'd had three kids by the time she was twenty-four.

I get it. I get why she had children so young. She wanted a family, and her own wouldn't do. She went out looking for what she should have had in plenty – but didn't – and that was unconditional love.

How great then, that in 1984 she married the comedian and performer, Keith Allen, a man famous for his narcissism and womanising.

Mum and Dad met through a radio show my dad did back in the 1980s called *Breakfast Pirate Radio*. My mum was a fan of the programme and she called up looking for work. Dad told her she could have a job if she could get him Ken Livingston on tape. Livingston was on the Greater London Council back then, and my dad wanted a fifteen-second clip of him talking. Mum, being the go-getter that she is, went out and got it. Dad was impressed. I think he was even more impressed when he saw her, this clever, dinky person with a Worzely Portsmouth accent and huge tits. He was, like, *Yes, please!*

Mum was young when she arrived in London. She had Sarah, a toddler, in tow, and she was studying at UCL so she was living in university digs in Bloomsbury. The artist Cerith Wyn Evans lived on the same block as her with his boyfriend, Angus Cook, and so did Lucian Freud's daughter, Rose Boyt, and the artist Celia Paul.

They all became friends – it was quite the scene – and Rose and Mum became close. She's one of my godmothers. Rose was in charge of the guest lists of the coolest nightclubs back then, clubs like Zanzibar and The Wag. She was tall with broad shoulders and there was no getting past her if she turned her back on you. It's why she was known as 'The Back'. She was 'The Back' and Mum was 'The Shelf'.

It was through Rose that Mum met Neneh Cherry and Andrea Oliver and her brother Sean, and they became a gang of friends. Alfie and I grew up with their kids: Naima,

Neneh's daughter; Andi's kid, Miquita; and Sean's kids, Theo and Phoebe. Phoebe's mum is Tessa Pollitt from The Slits. I was fascinated by them. They always had music in their house (Neneh, Andi and Sean were in a post-punk band called Rip Rig + Panic) and it always seemed like there was something going on in their house: a meal was being cooked or someone was getting their hair braided, relations were constantly visiting and if they weren't relatives they still seemed like family and were called Auntie. I spent a lot of time at Miquita's house. I loved it there because it felt like a community. Ours felt boring and lonely compared to theirs. At home I ate pasta with butter and cheese and watched TV, often by myself.

We're all still close. Miquita and Phoebe were bridesmaids at my wedding, and Theo runs our record label, Bank Holiday Records.

Mum and Dad's marriage lasted long enough to produce me and Alfie, but I don't think they were together much. They were both busy with their careers and their social lives. They spent time forming proper friendships with the people they were meeting rather than with each other. That's one reason I'm so close to my godparents and many of my parents' friends – because if we were spending time with my parents, then chances are it was when they were with their (usually separate) friends, too. I've got just one memory of Mum and Dad together as a couple. I was in Mum's bedroom and saw a man – my dad – in her bed. That's it.

Dad left when I was four. I didn't have much of a connection with him, so in one sense it wasn't a big event. The notion, cooked up years later, of me being 'Daddy's little girl' was invented by the media. Sometimes, I come across photos of Alfie and me as kids hanging out with our dad, but they were all set-ups: Keith Allen and his kids looking sweet together in go-karting jumpsuits! We didn't go go-karting with Dad: it was a promo pic for a documentary he was involved in. Keith Allen playing with his tots and holding one of them upside down! That was another work shot when Dad was in The Comic Strip – a group of comedians in the 1980s who became well known for their alternative take on comedy. I wasn't close to my dad growing up not because I was angry with him or punishing him – I didn't see enough of him to play out those feelings. I wasn't close to Keith because he wasn't around.

Soon after Dad left, Mum got together with Harry Enfield. They met at a dinner party given by my godfather, Danny Kleinman, a director my mum had met when she first came to London, and who is still one of her oldest, closest, proper friends – they were so close that Danny often felt like the dad I should have had. Harry felt like that, too. I think it's interesting that Mum knew that, for all Dad's anarchic socialism, what he really wanted was to be a rich and successful comedian. And here she was, moving on from Dad and moving in with the most successful comedian of the day. I accepted Harry straight away. I was like, *Well, if Mum is OK, then I'm OK.*

I did that as a child: I fell in with things. That's what you learn to do as a child if the two people you love the most appear to have disappeared on you. You become a people-pleaser because you're always guarding against further rejection. Rejection was the haze in which I lived as a child. My automatic response to any situation was: 'OK, OK, I'll do whatever you want, honestly, anything you want, as long as you stick around.' It's a response I fell into with men, too, as I grew older and began having my own relationships.

Harry wasn't just successful and well-off, he was kind and he was reliable. He and Mum were together for about five years, and while we lived with Harry, in a big, lovely house in Primrose Hill, he gave us stability and structure.

When we were kids, Mum was away, producing films a lot, on set or abroad. Films are demanding: they require a producer's full attention and pretty much all their time, and Mum gave her work her all. It was Harry who spent time with us and thought about what would be best, not just for him, but for us as children. Every Saturday he and I had a routine. He'd pick me up from the cooking classes he'd signed me up for, then we'd go shopping at Gap Kids and then have lunch together at our favourite Chinese restaurant.

Mum went away a lot because of her work, but that wasn't the only reason she was absent. When I was about seven or eight, she started taking drugs with one of her close friends. I guess it was kind of a phase of drug-taking in an *Ab-Fab*-hilarious-let's-get-out-of-it-darling sort of way. I guess.

Mum's friend lived on Talbot Road, near the Portobello Road. Portobello was a place where both my mum and I would end up spending lots of time, together and apart. I would later live on that corner with my godfather, Danny, and later with my boyfriend for a time, Seb, and again with another boyfriend, Ed. Different flats, same corner. You can see through the windows of all four properties from all four, so I feel like it's a locus for me, that corner; a central point in my universe – one of the ley lines of my life. It can't be coincidental either. It's one of those places that feels energetic to anyone who goes there, and it's a magnet for all kinds of people, rich and poor, black and white, old and young. It's around the corner from Portobello Market and all the energy that a vibrant market brings to a neighbourhood: it's there that you still go to find cheap vintage clothes and good records and delicious street food, and where there are all kinds of coffee shops and cafés and after-hours nightclubs, so the whole place attracts people who are, in some way, determined to express their individuality and nail down their style.

I loved West London when I was growing up. Sarah's patch was Islington, North London, and Alfie went to a Steiner school in North London, so he had his friends from there, but my friends, Jess, Phoebe and Miquita, and their families, had all moved west, and Portobello was our stomping ground.

I think Mum liked using her friend's flat as a place to escape to. She kept the fact that she was using quite separate from Harry. It's a way of convincing yourself that you are containing your habit, isn't it? To cordon it off into a different place or section of your life. It's also one reason why Mum travelled so much. *No, no, I'm fine, really – putting all this shit into my body isn't something I do in my real life, it's just a bit of fun I have in my parallel life, on Talbot Road, or when I'm away working. My wind-down. A way of coping with pressure. You know?*

I do know. I know how it all works because I did it when I was married to Sam. You try and hold it together when you're around your partner, but that's hard, and it makes you feel like you are suffocating, and so you plan yet another work trip away. The trips are legitimate and they are for work – you're not living a lie – but you do more than are necessary. You aren't being honest, either. You pay more attention to your work life in order to service your drug habit at the expense of neglecting your family, which makes you feel guilty so you plan more work trips to run away from your feelings of guilt. It's an exhausting, destructive cycle.

When we were young, Mum would return from her trips to America with stuff for us to open: packages of American sweets, stickers, Disney stuff, clothes from shops that weren't yet in London. It was guilt booty. I'd be excited about the presents, of course, but really what I was excited about was: *Mum's back! Mum's here!* But, all too quickly, she'd be off on another trip. That's what Mum did. I knew she went away to work and I accepted it, but I didn't know what else was going on back then. I understand it now too well. You leave your kids and that's painful. You feel guilty. You feel disengaged when you return. You don't know your kids as well as you should. Mothering them feels foreign and hard. It feels easier to keep escaping. One way to escape it is to drink or take drugs. Another way is to keep going away. Mum did both. So, later, did I.

I love Mum and I'll always preface any bad stories about her with how amazing and how tenacious she is, and how she's accomplished so much, because she is and has. We've been through some shit together, but here we are, decades later, and we're still really close. So some things went right.

But not everything. When I was eight years old, I went to a school in Camden called Cavendish. Mum had just started working as a film producer at Working Title, and though she got help with us kids, we didn't always have a proper nanny or someone taking charge. At pick-up time one day, because she was too busy taking drugs at her friend's house, she phoned up her office and sent a runner who was working there to collect me from school and bring me to her friend's. The runner had never met me before, but he did as he was asked. He ordered an Addison Lee car, got to the school on time, picked up Lily, took her to the Talbot Road address my mum had given him, and watched as she was buzzed into the flat. Then he returned to the office. Lily went into the flat where she found seven-year-old Alfie and his best friend, Theo, watching TV. She sat down and watched it with them.

Mum and her pal were there, but they didn't see or notice the kids. They were downstairs hanging out together. Meanwhile, moments after Lily had been picked up by the runner, Lily's mum arrived at the school to collect her daughter. Only she wasn't there. The runner had got the wrong Lily. The wrong Lily was at the Talbot Road house, but no one at the school knew this. All anyone knew was that this Lily had disappeared with a young man – no one had seen him before – into an Addison Lee car. Meanwhile, I was left waiting at the school. And though it wasn't so hard to unravel the mistake, nobody was answering the phone at my house (it was mostly landlines back in those dark days) because no one was there. They were all at Talbot Road, too busy watching TV or knocking back booze and drugs to notice what had gone wrong. It took a while, hours not minutes, to put things back to rights and restore the Lilies to their correct homes.

The incident didn't make me feel good. It added to me feeling like I didn't exist.

Not long after that, things reached a crisis point with Mum. I came home from school one day and she was in her bedroom with empty vodka and pill bottles all around her. She was crawling along the floor saying, 'The house is shouting at me to get out.' She was very distressed. I rang Harry. I felt like I was betraying Mum by ringing him when I saw her in that state, but I didn't know what else to do. 'Something's wrong with Mum,' I said to him on the phone. 'I'm scared.'

I finished at Cavendish after Year Six, when I was eleven, and somehow got a sports scholarship (I was quite good at hockey, it turned out) to a posh, sporty prep school in Somerset called Edgarley Hall.

I'd probably been up for the idea of boarding school because when I was about eleven, I began to read kids' books about the Second World War. I started with *Carrie's War* and then there was the book with that memorable title, *When Hitler Stole Pink Rabbit*, and, of course, I devoured *The Diary of Anne Frank*. But the ones that I was attracted to most were the ones about child evacuees.

It was the first time, as a child, that I felt like I identified with anything. Those stories chimed with me because I had this dream of being shipped off somewhere. These kids – even though it was horrible that they were yanked away from their homes and put on trains and sent to the countryside – what they got, at the end of the train ride, were mother figures that looked after them, cooked for them and encouraged them to play in the garden with other kids.

Edgarley Hall, however, was not the idyll I had imagined. I hated it there. It was too far away from London to go home very often and much too traditional. I didn't understand the references to 'Sloane Ranger' life and I wasn't familiar with the rituals that came naturally to most of the kids there: the jokes and manners and codes – a certain way of talking and eating and behaving – that you acquire if you grow up in a big house in the country with staff and ponies and dogs and parents who are rooted in the Establishment.

I felt isolated from the other kids and isolated from my family, and that feeling wasn't helped when I was left waiting to be picked up one Saturday afternoon. When you're at a boarding school like Edgarley, you get to go home for one weekend, twice a term. Those weekends, or 'exeats', one each side of half-term, are precious. There was a coach that ferried kids from Somerset to London so that the parents who lived in the capital or abroad didn't have to drive for hours to collect their offspring only to turn around and drive hours home. But when the coach arrived at the Royal Albert Hall, its designated London drop-off point, I was left waiting with the teacher for someone to pick me up.

No one did.

Mum had asked my sister Sarah to get me. Mum herself was too busy.

Sarah didn't show up. I felt humiliated and forgotten and

alone. The teacher's face was a picture: *Of all the children to be forgotten, it would be you.* Her witnessing my humiliation only added to it. I had to get back on the bus and return to Somerset.

Of course, later that night, my mum bustled around repairing the situation and trying to make good: she arranged for a family friend who lived near the school to come and pick me up the next day. That wasn't what I wanted, though. What I'd wanted was for her to get in the car and drive like the clappers that same night, however late it was, wrap me in her arms and take me home. The whole situation just seemed to confirm my feelings that Sarah and Mum had a special bond from which I was excluded. They were in London. I was away at boarding school, outside their magic circle. I wasn't allowed in. I'd always subconsciously resented Sarah because of her bond with Mum, but after that incident I had an actual conscious reason to resent her: she had forgotten me. *Everything was her fault.*

I also subconsciously blamed Sarah when Harry and Mum broke up in 1996, and we moved out of Harry's house and into a place in Islington. Sarah was badly behaved as a teenager. She was wild. Harry was the third father in her life and she'd already been failed by two. She was done by the time he came on the scene. All bets were off. She pushed every boundary she could. She looked older than her years and she was tall and thin and gorgeous. She was sexy and she was smart. People wanted her around. She could get into any club, go to any party, and so that's what she did.

I think Harry was patient for years, but he reached a

point where he gave my mum an ultimatum. It must have gone something like this: you've either got to deal with your daughter or I can't go on living with you any more, at least not like this. Mum interpreted this as having to make a choice between him and Sarah.

Obviously she chose Sarah.

Of course, their break-up was more complicated than that, but that's how I saw it.

Sometimes, Mum's heavy work schedule worked to our advantage. When I was fourteen, Mum's film *Elizabeth* started going into production. It became a big success and was nominated for seven Oscars, even though it hadn't been shot with a big budget or regarded as hit material with commercial appeal. It was a period story directed by an unknown Indian director, Shekhar Kapur, who Mum believed in, and it was Cate Blanchett's first big role outside Australia. Mum was in a good place when she was working on *Elizabeth*. She was clean and finding success. I was between schools, and so she arranged for me to travel around with her and be tutored on set.

I was proud of Mum, and I loved being with her in her world, even if she was too busy to actually hang out with us much. She was the boss on that film set. It was she who had put it all together and it was she who was running the show. No one knew what would happen with the film or how successful it would turn out to be, but you could tell that it was brilliant just day by day. Sarah and Alfie and I all had parts in the film as courtiers, but if I wasn't dressed up and on set then I'd hang out with the make-up artist, Jenny Shircore, who I'd known since I was little because she'd done lots of work with my mum and dad over the years. She looked after me. The hair and make-up people (they're nearly always women) are always the nicest to hang out with on a film set.

Mum liked hanging out with them, too. On Oscar night in LA, Eric Fellner and Tim Bevan, who run Working Title and were also producers of the film, didn't seat Mum next to them and Shekhar and the stars of the film. They put her and Jenny and Alexandra Byrne, who did the costumes, in seats towards the back of the room, even though all of them were nominated for Oscars. Mum didn't care. She was thrilled to sit with her friends and, in the end, Jenny was the star of the show because she was the only one who actually won an Oscar for *Elizabeth*. But I found it odd, looking at Tim and Eric, two men who'd rarely visited the set, sitting in what they regarded as the prime seats and taking all the credit.

There was one day on set that was stressful, it was a big production day with a lot going on. I think they were filming a complicated dancing scene at court, with Cate and Joseph Fiennes at the centre of it. I did something annoying on set. I can't remember what, but I distracted Cate and she snapped at me. Cate was nice generally, but there was a lot of pressure on her that day. It wasn't a big deal, except I was fourteen years old, and to me it was a huge deal. I was horrified and embarrassed. I went back to my mum's trailer and wrote a two-page apology letter.

Otherwise, I loved the experience of being on set with Mum while she was working, and I loved playing Lady-in-

Waiting 'E'. But not once on that set did I think that I'd want to become an actor. The fact is, I'm not a natural performer.

Being on stage with an audience doesn't come easily to me, and it's not the applause that gets me excited when I'm there. I'm not in my comfort zone up on that platform, not at all. What I love is seeing people connect with the lyrics I've written. When you see that people have memorised and then are singing words you've written, that's amazing – just seeing even one person respond to your words. The fact that I might also be entertaining them is an added bonus. It's *that* that gets to me, and makes me want to get on stage. But the stage is not where I feel at home. Of course, I could become a better performer. I could write bigger choruses or stick more catchy ear-worms into my songs or take more dance classes and learn about movement and writhe around the stage more, but that's not why I get up there.

I do it to sing songs I've written. Writing songs is cathartic, but nothing compares to someone else responding to them. That feels like a relief. When I write, what I'm trying to do is make sense of something in my life; often it's something that I've been unsuccessful at solving. So when people connect, it feels like they are saying, *Yes, I understand, and no, you are not alone, and it's OK, you aren't going mad, and yes, I've felt that way, too.*

I'm happier working it all out behind the scenes – I'm like my mum in that way. She does it by finding material and creating a team. I do it by writing and crafting a song. My dad is different. He's all about performance. He's a narcissist. He likes people looking at him for whatever reason – good or bad, either will do – *all* the time.

FATHERS

I didn't know much about Dad when I was young, except that he was an actor. He wasn't commercially successful. He was and is brilliant at what he does – writing, acting, comedy, stand-up – but he's a self-saboteur. I understand that, as I am, too. He was part of The Comic Strip in the 1980s, and I hear him get name-checked by comedians from that era as one of their heroes, but unlike many of them, he couldn't channel his comedic gifts into a proper career. He did this one-man show in the Docklands back then, when he came on stage naked and didn't allude to it for the first twelve minutes or so of the set, and people still talk to me about it. No one had done anything like that before. He was new and original and anarchic, but he couldn't sustain anything. Sustaining something takes work, after all. You can be brilliant once, but to keep doing it over and over is hard and intimidating, and that's what I think he was scared of: keeping it up.

Dad could be charming. He's clever. He was good-looking. When I think about him back when we were little, I mostly remember him driving us to places – he drove a Citroën – and then dumping us there. Anywhere, really: the juice and nacho stall in Camden run by a friend of his, say, or usually the Groucho Club. Occasionally, Alfie and I spent weekends in one of the hotel rooms at Groucho's, eating Toblerones from the minibar while Dad got smashed in the bar downstairs with his mates.

Groucho's was part of my life from a young age. I knew the phone number off by heart by the time I was six. How depressing is that? The name rings true for me too, because it really is a club I do not want to be part of, and yet they will have me as a member. God knows, I've spent enough time there over the years, enough even to be barred entry for a month at a time once or twice over the years, after being caught doing drugs in the loo. But when we were young, a room there was Dad's idea of childcare. Dad didn't do much of that – childcare, that is. Mostly, when it came to Dad looking after us, it was cancellations, crap excuses and disappointments.

He did once offer to help out my mum, when she was making her first film, *Hear My Song*. They were still together then. The film was made in Ireland and Mum took us kids there while she was working on it, enrolling us in the local school and nursery in Leixlip. I was four, Alfie was three and Sarah was ten.

'Alison,' I imagine he said, 'you're stressed out. I'm going to take the kids on holiday for a week to the South of France so you can get on with your work.'

'Thanks, Keith,' she must have replied, presumably surprised that he was kicking in. 'That would be a great help. Thank you.'

Dad had booked a hotel between St Tropez and Nice and, when we went up to our room, we discovered that his friend, Nira, who worked at The Comic Strip as the company's secretary, was staying in the room next door. They did the whole: 'Oh my God, how weird to see you here! You're on holiday? You on your own? Come and hang out with us,' thing, but there was no kidding Sarah.

Alfie and I bought into it. But Sarah knew. Dad and Nira were already having an affair. They'd planned the holiday so they could be away together. Soon after that, Dad and Mum split up, and we hardly saw Dad at all. Maybe Mum, angry, said, 'You're not seeing the kids!', or maybe he just didn't want to see us. Mostly, I remember him moving out of our flat in Bloomsbury and away from us, his family, and into a little flat on the Waldo Road in North-west London with a pig called Morris. It wasn't a dinky micro pig or one of those black pot-bellied ones either, but a real, fat Gloucestershire Old Spot-type, pink fucking *pig*. I trust that for a time at least they were happy together.

Dad didn't like it when Mum got together with Harry. He was horrible about him. He called Harry a dick. I know, Dad. You left Mum in a ditch with three kids to look after, and Harry, who everyone adores and who *doesn't* take cocaine, took on the family you abandoned without complaint. What a dick.

Dad and Nira got married when I was eleven. The wedding

was in a church on Haverstock Hill in Hampstead. Alfie sang, 'Where is Love?', from the film *Oliver!*. I sang the song made famous by Bette Midler, 'The Rose'. 'Some say love, it is a river,' the lyrics go, 'that drowns the tender reeds.' I'd just started singing lessons at school, and I enjoyed them immediately, though I had no idea yet that using my voice would become my calling. My grandad was sitting in the front row. He'd been a submariner in the Royal Navy all his life, spending months away at a time and under the sea, apart from his family. My dad's mum was Welsh and from a big, warm family, but his dad was from a strict English family who valued discipline above joy. He was short-backed, stocky, tough. Not a free-spirited man. Near him sat Damien Hirst, and just across the aisle was Eddie Izzard wearing thigh-high PVC boots. It was that kind of wedding.

The marriage didn't last. My dad wasn't faithful to Nira, either.

For example, when I was travelling in Thailand back in 2002, I met a girl on the beach and we got chatting. She said, 'You know what, I think you might know my sister, Tara. She used to hang out with your dad back in the day.' I remembered Tara instantly, the moment she said her name. Tara was the young woman who did the teas at the cricket games my dad took us to when he and Mum were still together. She had peroxide-blonde hair and wore bright red lipstick, and had a beauty spot on her face just like Madonna's. She was unbelievably sexy. Without thinking about it, I said to the girl, 'They were having an affair, right?'

'Yeah,' Tara's sister replied straightforwardly. 'That's right.'

I thought, *Well, there we are.* Even at three years old, I had known on some level that something wasn't right. But then you could probably mention any woman my dad has 'hung out' with and, chances are, if she's been up for it, they've shagged. It seems quite a lot of women were up for it. Shaggers do get laid, though, don't they? If you try it on often enough, you get some.

I think Dad has about eleven children in all. Or maybe it's thirteen. Or perhaps I'm exaggerating and it's eight or nine. I don't know. There's me and Alfie and my half-sister Teddie, whose mum, Tamzin, Dad has been with for fifteen years now. But there's a load more, some of whom are semi-official and others who we don't know much about, but who Dad has fathered just the same.

I do see my dad still, but I've learned over the years that everything is about him, so fine, that's the deal. I've stopped trying to fight or bustle about trying to find a spare slot in his universe. There isn't one. I'm sure when he thinks about how he fathered me, he thinks: *Well, I did a better job than my own dad. I wasn't cold or joyless. I wasn't a strict bastard. I was fun. I took my kids to the football and the cricket, even if I was getting my leg over with the blonde who did the teas. I was a laugh. I embraced good times.*

Dad would be right in many ways, if that's what he thinks. He compensated for what he'd lacked as a child and behaved differently from his own father. But it doesn't matter how funny someone is if they aren't around. Or, if when they are around, they only want the laughs to be directed towards them. Going to the football with your dad can be fun of course, but when, every time, you're the tagalong while he hangs out with his mates, the treat loses some of its value. I spent years trying to shout, *Dad! I'm* here. *What do I have to do to get you to look at* me? I never could. Whatever I did, however successful or however messy I became, either way, I couldn't get my dad to pay me attention, not as a child and not as an adult.

The penny dropped hard when I played at Latitude in July 2014. I was headlining that festival, which is a big deal, at least for most people. Festivals don't ask women singers to headline very often – more's the pity – and in fact I was only asked to do it at the last minute after the original headline act, Two Door Cinema Club, cancelled because their lead singer was ill. I was especially nervous because there had been press about how outraged some of the Two Door Cinema Club fans were, getting landed with Lily Allen instead of their favourite band.

Dad was at Latitude. He'd been in charge of organising their comedy tent for years, so he was a regular there. After Glastonbury, it had become his thing. He came to see me in my dressing room before I went on, but then said he had to go. 'Good luck!' he said. 'I'm off now.' I was gobsmacked that he was leaving. 'I've got my own responsibilities here, Lily,' he explained. 'A job to do in my own tent.'

'Dad,' I said. 'I don't think anyone at the Comedy Tent would begrudge you if you said, "You know what, guys, I know this is my tent but can you hold the fort for an hour or two while I watch my daughter headline this festival that we're all at?"' I was, like, 'I'm sorry, Dad, but I'm just not buying it.'

I remember thinking: *How the fuck am I meant to interpret*

him leaving, apart from something really fucked up going on? I was congratulated by people who *were* there watching me: my friends, my godmother Henrietta, my friend Matthew who sent me a text message as soon as I'd finished, saying how proud he was of me and how he'd been in tears watching me, and I remember thinking: *I want this from my dad, who was right here, a field away from me, but didn't come to see me perform one of the most challenging and important concerts of my career.*

That's what it's been like with Dad all my life. He has been there, around, in the same town as us, sometimes in the same building, but never with *us*. He was always downstairs in the bar with his mates or pursuing women or chasing drugs. What he wanted was attention, all the time. He wasn't interested in paying attention to us. Instead, we lived in the sidelines of his life, and there we have remained.

Presumably it's not coincidental, then, that one of the things I yearned for as I reached adulthood was to be the centre of attention. Ditto, you could surmise, my being attracted to older men, subsequent co-dependency, not being able to say no, and my habit of people-pleasing, as well as my disregard for authority. This last trait, partly due, I think, to my dad being unreliable as any kind of voice of authority, as well as it being stamped into my DNA, given that I am the daughter of an anarchist socialist comedian who didn't give a shit about anyone except himself (LOL), proved to be particularly unhelpful when it came to my education.

Hear My Song, my mum's first film, by the way, was a success. Diana, Princess of Wales came to the premiere. I was a flower girl and gave her a posy. Alfie had a box of handkerchiefs to give her, but somehow he got his knob caught in his trouser zip moments before meeting her. He was crying when she approached him.

'Are you OK?' she asked him.

'No,' he replied. 'I've got my willy caught in my zip.'

AN EDUCATION

I went to nine different schools in all. The first was a state primary called St Joseph's in Bloomsbury, while we were living in my mum's UCL digs. When we moved to a flat in Shepherd's Bush, Mum's friend, Siobhan, persuaded her to send us kids to private schools. Sarah and I went to Queensgate because that's where Siobhan's daughter, Jess, went. When Mum got together with Harry, they moved us to this ultra-traditional school in Chelsea called Hill House, where the kids wear a uniform of breeches and mustard-coloured socks so they look like they're going game shooting in Scotland. That didn't last long, and so I was moved to a more local primary school in Camden called Cavendish.

I liked Cavendish. It was there that I was first encouraged to sing. There was a teacher there called Rachel Santesso and it was she who first gave me singing lessons. Miss Santesso was great. I liked her a lot. I did my first solo at Cavendish too, and that was significant for me because it was something that I was chosen to do. For a child who feels invisible growing up, that's a big deal. The song was 'Baby Mine' from *Dumbo*. The headmistress at Cavendish was also a sympathetic person. She let me know, without making a big deal about it, that she was looking out for me. But Cavendish was a primary school, and it came to an end when I completed Year Six and was eleven years old. It was after that, that I went to board at Edgarley Hall.

I may not have liked Edgarley or stayed there long, but my time there was important in that the school took my singing ability seriously. At Edgarley, I had proper voice lessons that began with scales and learning how to sing arias, and ended, once the hard work was done, with singing something more accessible, like a show tune or songs from a musical. Because Edgarley was a sporty school, not many of the kids were into drama or singing, and so my singing stood out. There was another good singer there, though. She was called Olivia and she was in the year above me. She was blonde and tall and extremely pretty, and all the boys loved her. When we sang together in an assembly, she sang the song 'The Rose' and I sang 'Somewhere' from *West Side Story*. (That's why I chose to sing 'The Rose' at Dad and Nira's wedding. I didn't choose it for the lyrics, however apt they may have been, but because I wanted to knock Olivia off the top spot and claim her song as my own.)

Still, however envious I was of Olivia, it was me that was chosen to sing the solo in the school's Christmas carol concert at Wells Cathedral. The carol was 'In the Bleak

Midwinter' and never was a title more fitting, because on the way from London to Wells, Mum and Alfie had a car crash, and so it was a bleak night, indeed. (The carol also took on extra significance years later when I moved to Gloucestershire with Sam, because I discovered that Gustav Holst had been inspired to write the music by his childhood visits to Cranham, our nearest village.)

I'd assumed Mum and Alfie had been watching me from one of the pews in the cathedral, but when I got back to school with the rest of the pupils I was the only child whose family had failed to make it. I then assumed I'd been forgotten again, but just as I was starting my 'poor me' routine, Mr McGuire, the housemaster, took me aside. He explained that Mum had had to swerve to avoid a lorry driving dangerously in the middle of the road. Her little car had ended up on its roof in a ditch and she and Alfie had had to be cut out of the car and taken to hospital. Alfie was fine – shaken up, but not injured – but Mum had bitten straight through her bottom lip and she was being stitched up.

I felt awful when I heard this; I also felt jealous of Alfie. He had been in a horrible and frightening car crash, yes, but he had been with Mum and he was with her in hospital now. They'd been through an ordeal together and it would be something they'd share, while I could only hear about it from the outside.

I left Edgarley after two terms because I was unhappy; the somewhere else after Edgarley became a prep school called Dunhurst for a term and, then, when I was twelve, and September rolled around, it was Bedales.

Quite often, when I first became famous and one journalist or another wrote a take-down piece on me, one of their tropes was to accuse me of being a fake. Thought I was street? With my trainers and my London accent and my rough-girl, gobby opinions? Lily Allen, street? Lily Allen who went to a posh boarding school like Bedales? Who was I kidding? 'Over-privileged cry baby,' Julie Burchill flung out in 2011. 'Public-school tool,' she went on. 'They obviously do things differently at Bedales,' she said, to explain something I'd said or done.

I sometimes meet people who have been to Bedales and they look at me with a certain kind of wary admiration because my rebelliousness there has gone down in legend. 'We heard you put acid in the milk machine,' they say. But in fact I didn't do anything grand or dramatic like that at all.

In many ways, I should have fitted right in there. Bedales is known as an arty school and for attaching as much importance to the extra-curricular activities it offers – everything from photography to baking bread – as it does to the national curriculum it is obliged to teach. I continued singing there, and started learning to sing jazz – improvising and scatting with my voice while someone played the piano.

There was also a teacher there who I immediately took to. He was called Alastair Langlands and he taught English Lit and Classical Studies. He wasn't a young or groovy teacher – he was in his sixties and he wore breeches and tweed jackets, but he approached teaching as a kind of storytelling, which I loved. For his Classics lessons, he put whiteboards around the walls of the classroom and instead of wiping them down at the end of each class, he kept filling them up with the names of the characters we were learning about from Greek mythology and how they all connected together. That suited my memory, which works visually.

Similarly, for our English lessons, when he taught us *The Day of the Triffids*, written by John Wyndham, who had lived close to the school, Mr Langlands took us outside and into the landscape to read passages from the book, so we listened to the words while sitting in the very vegetation that had inspired Wyndham. That helped teach me that storytelling could be painterly and visual, and it's a lesson I use in my songwriting still. I don't want to write about a particular single feeling, or settle on one refrain in songs – '*Oh, my heart is broken; gee, how I love you…*', etc. Instead, I try and build up layers of details – it's Tesco carrier bags that the little old lady in 'LDN' is struggling to carry; it's his parents' basement where my URL Badman sits at his computer, in the song of the same name – to deliver a whole picture and tell a contained story.

Still, despite all this, I didn't manage to stay at Bedales for even a complete academic year, and while I was there I didn't do much work or make many friends with my own year group. This was because the summer before I went to school there, I'd been on holiday in Mallorca with Mum and her friend, Siobhan, and there'd been a whole gang of kids and teenagers there that I'd hung out with. One of the boys was going into his last year at Bedales. We'd made friends, and so once we got to school his friends became my friends. That didn't go down well with the other girls.

Boarding schools are run on hierarchies. Rituals and

privileges are crucial. You move slowly up the ranks to earn little freedoms like a toaster for your common room or later lights out or access to more television time, and it isn't done, if you're a new girl at the bottom of the school, to leapfrog straight into hanging out with the alpha boys in the upper sixth. I didn't care. Our gaggle of friends would hang out and smoke fags and, once a week, on a Wednesday afternoon, we'd go into town and buy a box of wine with the John Lewis store card that one of the boys had nicked from his mum's wallet. We'd then sit in the forest near the school, get drunk and let the boys finger us.

All this was fine, but two problems reared up as the school year went on:

1) it dawned on me that my cool, older friends, all in their last year, would soon be leaving, and I'd be left behind with the rest of the school who resented me. That made me feel extremely anxious. And 2) as June approached, the school said they wouldn't let me go to Glastonbury.

I went, anyway.

I think that's when Bedales were, like, *No, we can't have this person at our school any more.* By July, I'd been kicked out.

I wasn't going to miss Glastonbury.

By this point, too, I knew I could leave one school and start another – drifting between places was almost becoming a habit. I'd translate my feeling of utter disenchantment (which was, I think, about being a child full stop) into dislike of the particular institution I was at. 'This isn't right, Mum,' I'd say about whatever school I went to, and because she was busy in America and not very engaged with what was really going on, she'd just try to solve the immediate problem I was presenting her with. 'Of course, darling,' she'd say. 'You can leave and let's get you in somewhere else.'

I'm not saying I didn't deserve a pasting from Burchill. I probably did. And I did go to Bedales – for two and a half terms – but to define me by one of the many schools I went to, and never felt part of, was neither fair nor wholly accurate, and so I resented reading Julie Burchill's piece and how she diminished and belittled my work by saying I was handed it all on a plate. Keith Allen, posh? Britpop may have been about popular culture apparently unifying class differences, but that's exactly it: class differences. I was not born into the elite. Sure, I had media connections through my parents and an entrée into the Groucho fucking Club, but I managed to get a career in spite of that and my education – not because of them.

The latter certainly didn't provide me with any useful training or qualifications. I don't have any A-levels or a single GCSE. I didn't ever do any homework. I never learnt how. No one sat down with me to do it and so it just went undone, even though it became this ball of worry inside me, the homework I never, ever did.

That was part of the pattern of my childhood: the feeling of always being unprepared. For example, when I went to boarding school for the first time, all the girls had things like Tampax and deodorant. No one gave me that stuff or gave me the talk about how to look after yourself, even in the most basic of ways. I think that's another reason why I, as an adult, so quickly latched on to men and was, like, *You! You're going to look after me now!* As a child, I longed for adulthood, but as I got older, part of me wanted to remain a child so that I could fill up on what I felt had been missing from my life, and that was being looked after.

After I was expelled from Bedales, my mum tried to get me to carry on with my schooling. I went to a couple of London crammers, which are schools that teach the curriculum on an hourly basis without any pastoral care or the structure of a school day. They mainly service kids who have failed their GCSEs or A-levels, and need to cram on one or two subjects before their retakes.

Most of the kids at the crammer I went to were street-smart Londoners. I was fresh out of boarding school and though I'd felt too London for a country school, now that I was back in London, I felt like a country bumpkin. There was a bully at the crammer who picked on me from day one, and because I didn't know how to handle her, I told my sister Sarah and her best friend Emily about her. They both went to a London day school and had street smarts to a fault.

'What?' they said, all outrage. 'Some girl is giving you shit?'

The next day, they came into the college with me.

'Show us the girl,' they said, and I did.

'Are you bullying our sister?' they said into her face.

'No, no,' she said, suddenly intimidated.

'Say no again,' Emily said, clearly enjoying herself. 'Say it in my face.' She grabbed the bully's glasses and flung them on the ground, then ground them into pieces. They beat her up, not badly, but enough to frighten her.

The next day, the headmistress of the crammer, a woman called Julia, called me into her office.

'Were you involved in the incident yesterday?' she asked.

'No,' I lied. 'I had nothing to do with it.'

'I'm going to ask you that question again,' she said. 'And this time I want the honest answer.'

'No,' I repeated. 'I didn't touch her.'

She switched on the TV in her office then, and played me CCTV footage of Emily and Sarah beating up the bully while I stood by, watching and laughing.

That was my last day at the crammer.

'What are you going to do now?' Julia asked me, as she gave me my marching orders.

'I want to be a singer,' I told her. It was the first time I'd said such a thing out loud, and I didn't mean it in a serious way. I wouldn't have dreamt, back then, of claiming singing as something I was good enough at to pursue seriously. To me that would have been a kind of outlandish arrogance requiring the sort of confidence I didn't have. Singing? I hadn't even been to stage school. To be a singer, like a well-known singer? That was fairytale stuff as far as I was concerned. That was Whitney Houston being spotted in her gospel choir at church and then being introduced to someone famous and powerful like Clive Davis, who would wave his magic wand and make her famous. If that was ever going to happen in my world, it wouldn't be me who was spotted anyway, it would be the prettier girl, the blonder, taller girl… Olivia from Edgarley, say. But not me.

I didn't even harbour secret thoughts about it being my calling – not then. I knew I could sing. I knew, even, that I was talented at it, but I wasn't prepared to put myself on the line for it or work my arse off to improve at it. I'd never said to Mum, 'Look, it's actually the Anna Scher Theatre school or the BRIT School for Performing Arts that I want to go to, instead of another posh boarding school,' because whenever I thought about those places, I thought that I'd never get into those schools, and the last thing I wanted was to risk any kind of rejection.

So why did I say it? I said it because I had to say *something* and it seemed logical to give Julia my best shot; to lobby her with the only thing I knew I had excelled at: singing. I knew she wouldn't take me seriously, and I was right. Plus I knew I'd never see her again, so I wouldn't be held to my word, anyway.

Just as I thought, Julia looked delighted at my response. It was so easy to dismiss. 'If it hasn't happened by now, sweetheart,' she said acidly, 'it's not going to.'

Julia! I shouldn't have let my sister beat up someone and I shouldn't have laughed or lied, but whatever I didn't have (a sense of self, moral integrity, any kind of useful education, a single skill set), the one thing I had in front of me was time. I was fifteen years old! In theory, the *only* thing I had was plenty of time to become or not become a singer.

(Note: if you read my list of thank-yous on my first album, you'll see Julia's name on there. I thanked her for spurring me on. Her disbelief in me made me work harder.)

After that, it was no more school. My mum wouldn't let me sit around on my arse all day watching daytime TV, which I was prone to do, so I got a job as a runner at my godmother Henrietta Conrad's television production company, Princess

Productions. I didn't have any burning ambition to work in TV, but I didn't have *any* burning ambitions. Instead, I flitted from one thing to another over the next couple of years. I was a runner. I waitressed – I got a job bussing tables and clearing plates at a restaurant called Latymer Place and then at 192, the restaurant in Ladbroke Grove where everyone groovy in the media world met each other to exchange gossip, and network over lunch and drinks and dinner. It was like the Groucho Club of West London.

I'm not sure I was even paid to work at 192, but I knew an older girl, a waitress called Willow, who was the sweetheart of the restaurant, and who I had a crush on and wanted to attach myself to. I remember seeing Paula Yates there, who was eating what would turn out to be one of her last meals – certainly her last one in public – before she overdosed on heroin. You could tell she was in trouble when you looked at her. I had to talk to the police about seeing her, as part of their investigation into her death. She was joined at lunch by this guy that we all knew was a heroin dealer. They'd left together. It was the saddest sight.

But, despite my temporary occupations, what I'd said to Julia was not a random 'fuck you' remark. It couldn't have been. I may not yet have taken myself seriously, but saying something out loud is important. It meant that the thought of singing must have been beginning to lodge itself in my head just a tiny little bit. Mostly, though, when I thought about myself and my future, what I thought was this: *I'm seventeen years old and I've got no idea who I am or what I'm going to do with my life.*

But seventeen was an important age for me. It was that same year that I met two life-changing people. One was a man called George Lamb – we'll get to him. The other was Lester.

A LESSON

I met Lester through my best friend, Jess. She was friends with his cousin Becca, and they were part of a tight group of friends, siblings and cousins who hung out together in West London. They all descended, it seemed, from the same boho-aristocrat families that ruled groovy London life in the 1960s, and they all seemed to share the unmistakable combination of jaded entitlement and debilitating lack of purpose that marks out trust-fund kids. Lester's grandfather was David Ormsby-Gore, who went by the title of Lord Harlech. He was a legendary figure. Glamorous, urbane and clever, he'd been the British ambassador in Washington when JFK was president, and after Kennedy had been assassinated he'd been one of the men Jackie Kennedy had sought comfort in. They'd had an affair. His children, the Ormsby-Gores, were famous in the newspapers for being beautiful, racy and troubled, one of them dying young of a drug overdose. She had been Lester's aunt.

I was fascinated by this close circle of friends and relatives, many of whom had known each other all their lives, but I also felt like I was never really accepted by them. I didn't fit in. However much gilding my parents' media careers gave them, they hadn't been born posh and nor had I. Ostensibly that didn't matter, and Lester couldn't care less. We were the youngest kids in the group and we gravitated towards each other, then fell in love. But the issue lodged itself inside me. Even if I could ostensibly keep up with my new group of friends, I never stopped feeling like I was an interloper among them. How could I not? I was the only one who hadn't descended from the ruling class, and so I could never share their magic (and destructive) sense of power. I know now how insidious and unhelpful that belief is, and if I'd been a stronger person back then, with a more secure sense of self, I'm sure I could have batted away the group's collective ennui and air of superiority, but back then there was no denying that I felt fundamentally insecure around the people I was now spending all my time with.

Except Lester. I didn't feel insecure with him. When I met Lester it was, like, *Bang!* I felt as though someone saw me for the first time. I felt like a person. And though I attached myself firmly and immediately to him, it was then that I began to form my own identity and find my own voice – not outside in the world but inside myself – and that was important. That was a step.

Falling in love with Lester was monumental for me. It triggered so many things. Some were small but they were still important. The nits that had plagued me as a child and teenager disappeared. They just seemed to up sticks and vanish. (Apparently they don't like the pheromones that are released when you have sex.) As that was another thing that happened: Lester and I had lots of sex, and though I wasn't a virgin when I met Lester (more on that later), I hadn't yet explored sex with someone my own age or with anyone I loved and who loved me back. That was a big deal.

The way I handled the non-sexual physical side of things with Lester was telling. As soon as we got together, I stopped hugging and cuddling my mum and the rest of my family. I'm not a particularly tactile person, but I remember the comfort of being held and cuddled by my mum when I was little. I withdrew from that, not gradually, but actively and all at once as soon as I got together with Lester. I didn't want my mum touching me at all after that. I remember consciously feeling that that part of me had gone somewhere else, away from my mum and my family, and over to my man. It was as if I just decided that Lester was going to provide *all* the comfort I needed from then on.

I think that was the most significant aspect of my relationship with Lester: I replaced my family with him. I transferred responsibility onto him and I relied on him for all my emotional needs. After all, here at last was someone who actually wanted to spend time with me, rather than saying they were going to spend time with me but then fobbing me off.

I'd stopped working at Princess Productions by the time I met Lester. We started off staying at my mum's house in Islington, but then found our own flat in Ladbroke Grove.

I got a part-time job in a pub on Golborne Road. I was too young to serve drinks, but I cleared tables and stacked glasses into the washing machine, so I made a bit of money that way. My mum also gave me an allowance each week, so clearly I was relying on her for some things. It arrived in my bank account every Tuesday and it was enough for Lester and me to go out and buy an eighth of hash, two peach Lipton iced teas, a packet of fags, a copy of *MCN Motorcycle News*, and two Topics. Then we'd go back to our place, smoke our weed, drink our peach Lipton iced tea, eat our Topics and have lots of sex.

We were a couple of unformed kids – *such* kids – but back then I thought I'd arrived at adulthood. I took it for granted that Lester, this guy I loved, was my destination in life. I assumed we'd get married and have children together and I'd be with him forever. I believed that 100 per cent, grabbed that assumption with both hands and used it to define myself. It made me feel like I existed and had a path to follow.

In many ways, I feel like I had two childhoods. The first was the hazy, holding pen, invisible-feeling period of my actual youth, and the second was my time with Lester. Because *this* was the time that I started to discover what it was that I wanted. *This* was when people asked me what I was interested in and what I might like to do with my life. That's when I began to realise that I had to find a direction for myself, or at least have a kind of narrative: something to tell people when they asked about me.

Sometimes, I'd talk about how much I loved singing, but I didn't feel that I could channel that into work or anything too purposeful. Instead, I felt like my style was something that was beginning to define me. It was around this time that my interest in clothes ramped up, and finding distinctive (and cheap) things to wear from Portobello Market was an important weekly mission. I didn't think, *I'll find a career in fashion*, because I wasn't as far along in forging a direction for myself as most of my peers, but every time I went to the market and found some piece of clothing, costing almost nothing, which I felt I could make my own, it was like another piece of the jigsaw that depicted me had been filled in.

Because I was with Lester when I started to forge this sense of myself, of course being with Lester became inextricably linked *to* my sense of self. I was with Lester and we'd be together forever because *that was who I was now*. Even when Lester left me and it turned out that I could forge my own identity as a singer and songwriter, that idea of myself – being with someone, marrying them, having kids – remained imprinted inside me, as if underneath whatever garb I put on, there was this permanent toile of dependency that had formed around me when I found him and my world had finally tuned into full-colour focus.

Lester did leave. Thank fuck, looking back. After we'd been together for eighteen months, me working in the pub, and then at a couple of clothes shops, Lester set sail to travel the world with four friends.

I mourned his absence. I felt directionless. I moped about. I turned eighteen in 2003, and my only preoccupation was waiting for Lester to return to me in London from his travels round the world. Only Lester had decided, on his own, that he wasn't going to return to me.

★ ★ ★

Looking back, this was the first example of what became my *raging* co-dependency. Being co-dependent means you're addicted to being in a relationship: you cannot and will not be alone, no matter what. So, even if you are with someone who is damaging you or themselves – an alcoholic, say, or a drug addict, or someone who abuses you – you won't leave, because however misguided, being with that person (*especially* such a person) makes you feel needed and loved. They're dependent on you and you're dependent on them, and you're both dependent on each other's dependence. It's fucked up. But like any dysfunction or addiction it's real, and it rages through many of us.

I've never been locked in a relationship with an alcoholic or drug addict, like many co-dependents, but still, it's my thing: being with someone, always. I'll say what I think my partner wants to hear to make sure they'll stay with me. I'll do anything to make sure they won't leave. Sometimes, they leave anyway. Sometimes, it turns out the person you're dependent on isn't locked into co-dependency with you. In fact, they've grown tired of your neediness. They're done. They want to get the fuck out.

That was Lester. He was big time set on escape. He was on a boat in the Caribbean sunshine, and having to think about needy me waiting for him to get home was the last thing he wanted. He ended things over the phone. I had to pay for the call too, because that was the way satellite calls to mobile phones worked back then – they charged at both ends. At £10 a minute, it cost me hundreds of pounds to receive the news that Lester wanted no more of me. (It was some solace to realise that whatever it cost me, at least monetarily, it cost Lester, on the satellite phone, more.)

I couldn't cope when Lester rejected me. It didn't just feel like I'd lost my boyfriend, it felt like I'd lost my future. I also felt like I'd lost my friends. I no longer felt welcome among the people I'd been spending three nights a week with for the last eighteen months. I felt alone and lost, and I didn't know how to deal with those feelings at all. I wanted the feelings gone. I wanted and needed help going forward, but I felt like there was no one I could ask and I thought that no one would listen to me anyway, so what I did instead was cry out in the most dramatic and punishing way possible.

I took an overdose.

My mum found me (I had moved back home after Lester set sail), and got me to hospital. It didn't take me long to recover physically. The pills I'd taken were paracetamol, and Mum had found me in plenty of time. But it was clear that I needed help in all kinds of ways.

Mum thought it would be constructive to put me into The Priory. In many ways, while I was there, I made a full recovery back to the person I was before I took the pills: I returned to being Lily Allen, co-dependent, only minus the actual dependent, and I had a plan to fix that.

I was going to find Lester and get him back.

I had just enough in my savings to buy a plane ticket to

India, because I knew that Lester was headed there at some point. If I went there, ostensibly to see the sights, recover myself, and hang out, chances were, I told myself, I'd just run into him somewhere on the hippy trail of Southeast Asia. I thought I could get information on where he was going on his own sailing trip by studying his Facebook page, but he wasn't very good at updating it.

It would be a gap-year trip – without knowing what my gap was between. I had neither just left school nor had plans to go to university.

I didn't find Lester… of course not! Sometimes, when people ask me about the trip that I took alone (me, alone, out in the world?), I say, 'Oh, it was good. I met people out in India and Thailand, and had a good time. I read a lot and saw the Taj Mahal and got quite drunk, and generally hung out in beautiful places.' But the trip was a disaster. The truth was, I'd had a horrible time. The truth was, I hadn't been able to look after myself at all, and felt, more than ever, that I couldn't survive on my own in the big bad world. Thank God, then, that at least I'd already discovered an alternative world I could escape to, and, it would later turn out, inhabit and make my own.

Thank God for the world of music.

MUSIC

didn't grow up in a house filled with music. My mum had a few records because some of her friends were musicians, but she didn't play them. She didn't own a record player. I discovered music when I was ten and my dad took me to the BBC for a recording of *Top of the Pops*. As I left, the producer gave me ten CD singles from the show. The songs weren't great: they included 'Cotton Eye Joe' and a song by Ace of Bass and another by Des'ree, but there was also 'Over My Shoulder' by Mike & the Mechanics, which is a song I still love. But having that music all to myself blew my mind. I listened to those CDs over and over again. They opened the door into this other world where expressing yourself and what you felt or desired or longed for or loved flowed naturally into song.

When I went to boarding school, I was given a Spice Girls' album, which I loved, and that was my record collection: the album *Spice* and those *Top of the Pops* singles. It was enough to get me hooked.

On a school trip to Naples I sat next to a boy on the coach I didn't know very well before the trip. He had his own Case Logic (remember those?) full of music. 'Have you heard this?' he'd say, and give me an album by Cast or a song by Ash or play music by Pulp and Blur. He introduced me to Britpop, and he had a collection of Ministry of Sound compilations (I couldn't make sense of it when I listened to them), which he declared the coolest ever.

From then on, music was in my life. There was no single 'eureka' moment of, like, 'Oh! Music is my thing now...', but listening to it became something I did. I listened to songs and I could learn them quickly and easily. I'd save up for CDs. I'd put on my headphones at school and sing along to Oasis and Lauryn Hill and The Roots and Erykah Badu. I got the soundtrack to Baz Luhrmann's film *Romeo + Juliet* and I loved that. I'd know immediately if I liked something – I could connect to a song's melody instantly. I listened to Finley Quaye (my mum played him on holiday, probably after reading about him in the *Guardian*), TLC, Mary J. Blige, and Aaliyah. (My sister and her friends were into R&B.)

I started going through my dad's record collection and discovered punk and reggae. For Christmas, when I was fourteen, Dad bought me a pair of decks and I learned to use them in his flat in Holloway. While I was playing his old reggae sevens and falling in love with ska and hip hop, my friends Miquita and Phoebe were discovering rock music and grunge. They loved Nirvana and Hole. When we started going to rave parties every weekend and taking drugs, drum and bass became our common ground.

Meanwhile, my dad and his friends, Alex James and Damien Hirst, had formed the band Fat Les. They'd written and recorded a song called 'Vindaloo' for the English national football team, which became an unofficial anthem for the 1998 World Cup and reached number two in the charts. Suddenly, there was cash about and the music studio became a fun place for Dad and his mates to meet up and hang out and take coke. Dad and Alex James were spending lots of time together – plenty of their mates came and went with Fat Les, but they were the ones behind it all. I used to go and see them sometimes, because going to the studio (or the football) with Dad was a way for me to try and establish more of a relationship with him. Sometimes, he'd ask me to sing backing vocals on a track, and slowly and gradually that led to him saying, almost casually, one day, 'Look, I've got you this thing that we can do together. You can sing on a record that I'll put together, and I'll wrangle a deal with a record label.'

The deal that Dad got was with a record company owned by Warner called London Records, but I don't think he did it just as a way to make money. I think the idea to make a record together was a way for Dad to show that he loved and believed in me. I think it was his way of trying to give me something. I think it came from a nice place. I think. Other times I think maybe he got a big finder's fee and signing up his seventeen-year-old daughter to be a singer *was* about cash, but mostly I dismiss that thought and go with the nicer, better, sweeter version.

That's how I got my first record deal – it was an act of nepotism, pure and simple. I got it entirely because of and through my dad. Dad and a musician friend of his called Pablo Cook wrote most of the songs together. Pablo was the producer of the record, and a woman called Octavia was the A&R co-ordinator with the record label. The songs were folksy, or sometimes we'd do a cover version of a song we thought might work.

It didn't work out. None of it felt right or like it ever clicked; not the songs or us working together, or even my voice. London Records lost interest in us pretty quickly. Nothing was said, but, while we were working, things began to be whittled away. Pablo would email Octavia asking what the budget was for strings, say, and the reply would come back saying, *There isn't a budget for strings, do without.*

It became less fun. It didn't feel like it was going anywhere and it certainly didn't feel like I was pursuing my dream. I felt like I was in Dad's dream. I had two managers then – it's pretty standard to get a manager when you sign a record deal, just as you also get a lawyer – and when things started to fall apart, they told me that I'd have to sue London Records to release myself from the deal, even though it was clear that London Records had zero interest in, or enthusiasm for, me. This was standard procedure, I was told – a way of closing a contract.

Only it didn't feel so standard when in response to me trying to leave them, London Records sent me a letter saying they were going to counter-sue me for £3.6m for breach of contract. I remember reading that letter and feeling scared and completely discombobulated. The amount, £3.6 *million*, was such an abstract figure. It had nothing to do with me or my life or anything I could grasp as within my ken.

It was, like, *You what? You're suing seventeen-year-old me for how much?*

Mostly, I tried to ignore it. I shoved the letter away, under the bed. That's what I did with money-related worries, and what I continued to do: I shoved them aside. I stashed paper bills and demands for payment under my bed for real, but it felt like there was a monster lurking under there, too.

Mum was immediately dismissive of the letter. 'That's absurd,' she said. 'How are they going to sue you? You don't have any assets. What are they going to take?'

Mostly I thought: *I'm done with this. I'm not a singer anyway.* Hadn't I always been scared of declaring myself a singer? Well, I'd been right. I'd tried to sing, and I'd been rejected.

I thought, *Fine, I'm done.*

Mum was adamant that I wasn't going to go back to waking up every day with no routine and nowhere to go, and so between us we came up with the idea that I should go to floristry school. It was a great plan. I loved flowers and working as a florist felt like something I could do. I did it, too. I followed through. I took a floristry course at a school in Hackney and I completed it. I loved it. I was with Lester then, so I'd go to floristry school and do my shifts in the pub and smoke weed and hang out with him. That was until Lester left and I then, of course, was, like, *Who am I and what am I doing?* and because I didn't have any answers or ideas, I thought, *Oh, I must be nothing,* and I ended up taking too many pills and being admitted to a mental hospital.

It was while I was in The Priory in early 2004, being treated for depression, that I got the call from my managers saying I was now officially off their books. The lawyers had wrangled me free. I was no longer under threat of being sued. I was a free agent, up for grabs. Lily Allen: seventeen years old, in rehab, having failed at work and love, with nothing but a floristry course and a load of legal proceedings on her CV.

I put the phone down, nonplussed. *Whatever.* It rang again immediately. It was George Lamb, a man I hadn't spoken to for a year and a half. 'I'm calling to see what's going on in your music career,' he said, perfectly cheerily.

'Nothing,' I told him. 'I've just been dropped.'

'Oh, good,' he said. 'Perfect timing. Why don't I take you on and be your manager?'

WORK,
PART ONE

met George Lamb in Ibiza, the summer before I fell in love with Lester.

Every August, my mum and her friend Siobhan took all us kids – me, Sarah, Alfie and Siobhan's daughter, Jess – on holiday to a house they rented in Deiá, Mallorca.

That year, in the summer of 2002, Jess and I and a bunch of other kids left our mums in Mallorca and got on the ferry to go clubbing in Ibiza for the weekend. I liked Ibiza, and I knew it a bit because I'd been there with my mum two years before when she was working there on a TV film.

That August weekend I didn't return to Deiá with Sarah, Siobhan and Alfie. I'd fallen in love with raving and clubs, and I'd decided I'd have more fun if I stayed in Ibiza by myself.

I found a room at a Welsh hostel in San Antonio, which I shared with some random guy, and I got a job at a record shop called Plastic Fantastic, which also sold tickets to the big clubs on the island. Part of my job was pushing the tickets in the shop or, better still, outside on the main drag in San Antonio. As a side venture, I set up my own little business selling ecstasy; after all, if someone wants four tickets to Manumission, chances are they'll also want a couple of Es. I was their one-stop shop. Fuck knows how I got hold of the Es in the first place, except that it's Ibiza, isn't it – there's always someone with a hundred Es in their back pocket happy to sell them to you.

I didn't make much money from it, though, and what I did make I mostly spent on clubbing. I had a lot of fun that summer. But between the drugs and the late nights and not sleeping much, things also got out of hand. There were various mini-dramas, which I always embraced. I seem to like having a bundle of dramas to carry around. For example, I was booted out of my room at the Welsh hostel for not paying my bill so my drama that night became, *Where the fuck am I going to sleep?* The problem was solved when I ran into a DJ I knew a bit called Jon Ulysses who said I could stay on his sofa once he'd finished his set at a club called Es Paradis.

That night I took my suitcase to Es Paradis, and got talking to a guy called George. He told me he was working the season promoting the club, Space, and had rented his own place for the summer. He saw my suitcase and asked me where I was staying. 'I've been thrown out of my hostel,' I told him. 'But it's OK because Jon Ulysses has offered me his sofa. I'm staying with him tonight.'

'No, you're not!' George said. 'Not on your own. Jon Ulysses is a perv. Look,' he continued. 'Come back and stay with me.'

George was fit and quite a bit older than me. He was exactly my type. I assumed he was making a pass at me. I thought I was in.

But George didn't come on to me. He took me back to his house and made up a bed for me on his sofa. When I woke up the next morning, he poured me a cup of coffee. 'I hope you don't mind,' he said, 'but I went through your phone while you were asleep and called your mum. I told her that I don't think you should be here any more. I'm going to take you to the airport and put you on a plane back to London.' And that's what he did.

It was an amazing thing. It was one of the first times a man had done something nice for me without any sexual agenda.

George was a life-changer. I didn't know that then, and I didn't think about him much after that, but he held on to my number and nearly two years later he rang me at exactly the moment I needed to hear from him, then helped reset me on my track forwards.

Sometimes, you meet the good guys.

George and I began to hang out together once he took me on and became my manager. He took me to Yo Yo, a club night at the Notting Hill Arts Club, which was the hangout place for people in the music industry then. That's where I met Seb Chew, an A&R guy and producer, who is now my best friend, creative director and soulmate. He's the person I speak to five times a day, and the man I trust most in my life. I rely on Seb in all kinds of ways, in my work life and as a friend, but I'm not dependent on him, not any more.

Of course, back when I first met Seb and we became friends, I attached myself to him in every way I could – romantically and sexually being the most adhesive and effective, or so I thought at the time – because that's what I always did. *It's your turn, Seb, to look after me* – that was more or less the only option I gave him for a time. But in fact, though we were boyfriend and girlfriend for a short while, real friendship is what lies at the core of our relationship. It started at Yo Yo where I'd go every week, sometimes with George, but more often with Miquita and Phoebe. We'd wear cropped Nike sports tops and Stussy jeans with trainers and chunky gold jewellery. We'd dance and get drunk and take drugs and gradually got to know this group of record-industry boys who all seemed to be from West London.

George didn't want me to be a party girl though, or even just a singer. He told me I should write. 'Look,' he said. 'I hate to break it to you, but this business is not really worth it if you don't write your own stuff, especially as a female artist.' He was right. At that time, in the early 2000s, there weren't many female solo artists around. Mostly the appetite was for boy groups playing twangy guitars. The Libertines had made it big. So had Razorlight. Coldplay had become massive. On the more manufactured pop side, it was all about groups put together by managers. Girls Aloud, who had met on a TV talent show in 2002, was becoming a big deal.

'OK,' I said to George, not thinking about it much. I'd always kept notebooks, after all, and written down my thoughts and yearnings. 'OK,' I said again, blagging it. 'I'll write.'

After that, George sent me to Manchester to work with a couple of producers he knew who called themselves Future Cut. I drove there in a car I'd bought at a car auction in Chelmsford. It was a crappy, beaten-up little Peugeot 206, but I loved it. People used to leave notes on its windscreen, saying things like: 'Your car is hilarious, can I buy it?' I didn't care. For me, that car meant independence. It was a ticket to my future. It was like a partner, but more reliable. It was there waiting for me, even if it didn't always start up very well.

I was ready for Manchester, it turned out. I had a load of mix tapes I'd made full of my musical reference points, and I could stay with my dad's friend, Bez, who had been in the Happy Mondays, and who lived in Glossop. It was kind of crazy there. Bez and his wife, Debs, who I loved, had got divorced and Bez had a mad girlfriend called Heather. They used to fight a lot. To earn my keep, I got up early every morning and helped with Bez's kids, taking them to school. When I got back, Shaun Ryder, who lived next door, had usually wandered in for his cup of tea wearing just his underpants. Often we'd open the post together and stare at the bills, most of which were red. I remember thinking: *But, Bez, you were in the Happy Mondays. How could you be broke?*

I know the answer to that one only too well now.

After I'd dropped Bez's kids at school, I'd drive to New Mount Street, where Future Cut had set up a tiny studio in one of those community buildings that are divided into cheap work units. It was a crappy, makeshift place to work but we didn't care. We got on with it.

VOICE

I wrote 'Smile' on my first day. It took about half an hour. I started singing Britney Spears' lines, 'Oh, baby, baby, how was I supposed to know,' over some chords, then replaced those words with my own. Then I wrote more words and found my own top line, which became the melody. That song, about Lester breaking up with me, was inside me. All I had to do was let it out.

I know this sounds improbable. George told me I should write, I said I'd give it a go, he sent me to Manchester to work with a couple of great guys, and out came 'Smile'. But that is how it happened, at least as a sequence of events. Of course, nothing is that simple. Nothing comes from nowhere. But in another sense, I'd been slowly forming my songs inside me for years. My childhood of silence (at least metaphorically, if not always literally) meant that when I discovered music it felt crucial to me as a way of open expression and it gave me forms to follow (verse, chorus, verse, repeat chorus and so on), which meant there was a kind of containment for all my sprawling feelings and thoughts. All I needed was a studio and out those forms came, little fragments of what I thought and felt and had seen and observed. My time with Lester and the time I'd spent hanging out in West London, being in love, getting rejected, feeling insecure, having Alfie as a brother: all these things provided me with my subject matter.

I'd learned so little at school, but I had been taught to sing. I'd sung with my dad and it hadn't worked out, but still, I'd used my voice. It had been part of my training, even if I hadn't realised it. I'd held tunes and I'd found out that if I didn't connect with a song then I wasn't able to sing it. I'd discovered music and had spent hours and hours and hours putting together playlists and songs, juxtaposing one song with another depending on what felt right, or to create a mood or usher a surprise. Music had become my thing. I'd get up in the morning and that's what I'd do: listen to music and discover new stuff. My friends and I were part of the first generation of kids who accessed music digitally, so it wasn't like you had to save up to buy an album which you then listened to over and over again. We did that with our iTunes accounts, of course, but we could also endlessly explore every kind of sound on file-sharing sites like LimeWire. The mix tapes I'd made were full of my musical reference points. These were varied, to say the least. Blondie was on there, and The Streets, drum and bass, lots of different ragga dancehall and ska, and old Phil Spector Wall of Sound tunes.

The second song I wrote was 'LDN'. That came easily, too. I'd spent all this time in London sitting in Falafel King or in cafés on the Portobello Road or on the bus or tube, watching people and how they interacted with each other. I'd fill in the gaps and create stories around the people I saw, making up conversations I imagined they'd be having, as if I was watching a movie that I was making up as I went along. I'd think about what their houses looked like, or whether they had kids, and what they'd have for dinner. I had this fantasy thing going on all the time in my head, and once I started writing, it all came out.

Still, however naturally songwriting came to me, I had a lot to learn. After we'd written the verses and chorus for 'Smile', Tunde, one of the guys in Future Cut, was like, 'OK, great, let's do the middle eight.'

I was all: *What the fuck's the middle eight?* I had to sneak off and call George to ask him, so that I didn't reveal my complete ignorance in the studio.

'It's that bit in the middle that links two sections of a song,' George told me.

That's why the middle eight in 'Smile' goes: 'La la la la la la.' It's because I didn't know what else to write. Back then, I was feeling my way into songwriting. It was like an experiment. I felt like, *Well, I've already failed at this singing lark, but here I am making up tunes. How wrong can it go?* I felt like I had nothing to lose.

I felt free and unrestrained writing those first songs; unselfconscious and unhampered by expectation. It's a gift to work like that, without any pressure or expectations or anyone trying to make you repeat a formula, which is what happens when you find success with a song or album.

Plus, the guys from Future Cut took me seriously. They added their own chords and helped me construct the songs properly, but they liked what I was doing enough to build on it. That was new to me, and revelatory. I began to think, *I wonder if I can be myself* and *make music that I like, and for it to actually work?* I didn't want my songs to sound like anyone else's.

I think part of the reason that my music felt different was because I wrote without knowing any rules. This can result in originality and it means you aren't easily pigeonholed, which is a good thing, but it comes with its own in-built problem too: if your music doesn't sound like other people's, then mostly record companies aren't interested in it.

I wrote five songs with Future Cut over two weeks in the autumn of 2004: 'LDN', 'Smile', 'Knock 'Em Out', 'Take What You Take' and 'Friend of Mine'. All of them made it onto my first album. Two of them, 'Smile' and 'LDN', would go on to become big hits, selling nearly a million copies between them.

But, at first, no one wanted them. They were rejected by everyone. By Christmas, I had those five songs in my pocket to shop around with, and a manager to get me through the right doors. But I could not get a record deal.

Frankly, I wouldn't have signed me, either. I wasn't just Lily Allen, writer of a handful of reggae-inspired pop songs. I was Lily Allen, Keith Allen's daughter who'd been dropped by London Records, and who was now being managed by

George Lamb, a newcomer no one in the business had heard of or knew.

I was also, in the small world of the record industry, Lily Allen, Seb Chew's girlfriend. Seb was working at Polydor then, and he'd signed the Scissor Sisters and Feist and Rufus Wainwright. He was smashing it. Plus, he ran Yo Yo, where all the A&R guys hung out. No one was desperate to take on Seb Chew's girlfriend. It was easier to steer clear of something that in all likelihood wouldn't work out, than risk pissing off Seb. And it wasn't as if I was bowling around town going, 'Hey! I've got five amazing songs under my belt here!' either. The confidence I'd found in Manchester working with two guys in a small room had quickly evaporated on my return to London. I genuinely didn't know if what I'd written amounted to anything good or substantial.

'It might be time to pack it in and move on, Lil,' Seb said to me, after George and I had done the rounds and been rejected. He had a point. We'd tried and it hadn't worked. No one was interested. George politely let himself go as my manager, and I moved on, too… by hook and by crook, in the right direction.

Through George, I had a new lawyer called Kieran, and through Kieran I met Adrian Jolly, who was on the junior rung at Empire Management. They took me on and, in the autumn of 2005, I landed a deal with Parlophone.

It was an atrocious deal. Parlophone signed me up for £25,000. That is, £25,000 for *five* albums. That's a low-investment, low-risk deal for them, and it showed how little Parlophone valued me when they took me on. But they were busy, so it wasn't like I was this hot new project for them to work on. They'd just put out Coldplay's album *X&Y* and *Demon Days* by Gorillaz. They had organised an All Saints comeback too, so they had that to manage. They had big fish to fry. Lily Allen? The guys at Parlophone were, like, *Who the fuck is Lily Allen?*

But Lily Allen had the bit between her teeth now. Lily Allen had discovered a social media platform called Myspace and was using it to develop her voice. Lily Allen was beetling away, building up her profile and putting her songs out into the ether.

It was the rapper Lady Sovereign who told me I should put my music on Myspace. I met her at a party and we got talking and she told me there was this way I could take control and put my stuff out there without waiting for my record company to notice me. Her advice felt important to me, and it became defining. This wasn't a push-up from my dad or my boyfriend. It would be me taking control of things; me being responsible for creating a space for myself and for getting my music heard. I was up for the graft of it. 'If it's good,' Lady Sovereign said, 'people will listen to it. They'll tell others, too.' She was right. I set up my account and put up the songs I'd done with Future Cut.

Then I did a song with Greg Kurstin, and I put that up, too. Greg Kurstin is an American musician, songwriter and record producer; these days he works with people like Adele and Sia and The Foo Fighters. He's huge. Even in 2005, he was already massively respected in the music industry. Parlophone wouldn't have hired him back then just to work with me. I was much too small. They hired him to work with All Saints, whom they'd re-signed for a million quid soon after I got my lousy deal. (That had put things in perspective pretty quickly. A million quid for a comeback? I was livid. I couldn't believe it.)

If you've signed a group for that much money, you don't ignore them and let them get on with it. Parlophone hired All Saints a big, beautiful studio in Primrose Hill and flew over Greg Kurstin from LA and paid for some serious session time.

The problem was, the girls didn't show up at first. So Parlophone were like, *What about that person we signed recently for pin money? Oh, yeah, Lily… get her down there to work with Greg while we round up All Saints.*

Greg and I hit it off. We started writing the song, 'Everything's Just Wonderful' the first evening I went to the studio. We finished it the next morning.

I immediately put it up on Myspace. The record company didn't care what I was doing because I was barely on their radar, and this suited me just fine.

I made mix tapes with Seb, too. They had my songs on them, but mixed in with songs by artists who'd influenced me: The Specials, Jay Z, Blondie and others. I did two, each with a run of two hundred, and I made the covers by cutting out bits of card and spray painting them with their titles: My First Mix Tape, My Second Mix Tape. (My mum's living room floorboards have still got paint marks on them from my artwork.) I put the homemade CDs up on my Myspace page, along with a message: *Does anyone want one of these?*

I wrote a blog, too. People read the blog, they ordered

the mix tapes and they downloaded the songs. They told their friends about me, and as 2005 turned into 2006, my Myspace traffic began to ramp up. Things started exploding. The songs were being downloaded thousands of times. I had tens of thousands of 'friends'. With the help of Parlophone, I issued one of my demos, the song 'LDN', as a 7-inch vinyl and pressed 500 copies. They sold out immediately.

I was beginning to feel excited, and a bit more confident. I knew from my parents how quickly things in show business can turn around. I also knew from my London Records experience that early promise can lead to nothing and that projects can get so far and then be dropped. I knew from my relationship with Lester and my own parents' histories that people might love you one moment, but forget about you the next (or hate you). But still, I began to think that when it came to my music, I *wasn't* just blagging it. I began to think: *This is what I'm supposed to be doing.* I began to think: *This is something I can do.* I began to think: *I'm a singer. I write songs. I'm doing what I should be doing.*

In the spring of 2006, a young journalist from the *Observer Music Monthly* (OMM) contacted me through Myspace. She was called Rosie Swash and she emailed me saying that she wanted to write a little piece about me. She asked me to send her some press photographs she might be able to use to go with the piece.

'I can't,' I replied. 'I haven't got any press photos.' I didn't have anything like that, and Parlophone was still largely uninterested in me, my music or my Myspace activities. Instead, between us, Rosie and I organised a mini photo shoot in my mum's house. There was no stylist or make-up artist. I wore what I was into at the time, which was prom dresses with trainers and big, chunky, gold jewellery.

Once they'd read Rosie's piece, the *Observer Music Monthly* decided to follow up with a bigger feature. The editor of the magazine, Caspar Llewellyn Smith, called up Parlophone. 'Can I talk to whoever looks after Lily Allen?' he asked. 'We want to put her on our cover.'

No one was looking after me then at Parlophone, but Caspar was put through to Murray Chalmers, who worked in the publicity department and was the go-to person for anything press-related. Murray and I would go on to work together for eleven years, but back then he was, like, 'Lily who? Hang on a minute.' Then he walked round the Parlophone office knocking on doors and interrupting people at their desks.

'Anyone know who Lily Allen is?' he asked.

'Yeah,' someone said. 'We signed her a few months back.'

'Oh,' said Murray. 'Well, *OMM* want to put her on their cover this weekend.'

And that's when things started moving. *OMM* put me on the cover of their May 2006 issue. Miranda Sawyer wrote the piece. It was celebratory and accurate. We got on and she seemed to understand what I was about. And now, so did Parlophone. All of a sudden they were, like: '*Oh, it looks like we've got an album here and we should be running with it. Let's get Lily and Greg back together to finish it off, let's get it out and make some money!*'

Who is Lily Allen? Oh! We've got Lily Allen. Hel-lo, Lily Allen!

FAME

Fame, if you're a popular star in the entertainment industry, is a game. At least, it is and it isn't, depending on your levels of sanity and detachment and how well planted your feet are in the ground. It's easier than you'd think to stray onto a slippery slope, and start to believe that it all matters and that you've been anointed for a reason: that you are, actually, truly deserving, and that the blips in the fame bubble – the squabbles and hurts, the disses and put-downs – are urgent dramas that must be attended to and redressed. *God forbid*, you think when you're in the bubble, *that it might ever burst.*

Sometimes the hurts are real. Being pursued by the paparazzi feels threatening. At the height of my fame, I'd get up and the first thing I'd see when I looked out of my window was a wall of men – twenty, thirty of them – sitting outside my flat, watching my door and waiting for me to emerge so that they could follow me *everywhere* I went. That was intimidating and made me feel paranoid. Having your home turned into a prison is unfair. Likewise, getting bullied by tabloid journalists is upsetting. Dealing with online trolling is distressing.

A lot of the time, even when you are firmly inside the fame bubble, you know how absurd it all is: a gossamer illusion. You know you're Alice and you're through the looking glass surrounded by Mad Hatters and Tweedledees and Dums – fellow celebs and hangers-on, photographers and tabloid journalists: everyone there not because it's important or edifying, but to make a buck. Wherever you turn there are women-baiters prodding away, trying to get you to say stuff – shit about other celebrities preferably, especially if they are younger and prettier than you. That's, like, top scores in the celebrity bear-baiting game. But even when you *know* it's all smoke and mirrors, you still sometimes take it seriously. You can't help yourself.

There are two reasons for this. One is that it's easy for any of us to take ourselves too seriously. We're all prone to vanity and self-importance, and it's easy to lose perspective when you've been flattered to believe that everything revolves around you. When that happens, tiny problems can become amplified into ridiculous dramas. I mean, does it actually matter where you are sitting at a fashion show or what your billing looks like on a festival poster? No, it does not.

Believing yourself to be hot shit needs to be sorted out. Often when you read an interview with someone famous, they'll say that it's their family or their long-term friends that keep them grounded. *Yeah, yeah, great that you're number one, but the dog has become epileptic so that's what we're dealing with here in the real world*, they might say, by way of explanation about what happens when they go home. Bump, they're back, and reminded of what's important: family, health – real problems happening in real time that require real attention.

One of my problems, though, was that my family and friends didn't bring me down to earth much. I'm not passing the buck. I know it's not their job to wait on solid ground so as to provide anchorage for me when I'm ready to do less flying about. Fuck that. Maybe some people get into the bubble and think, *You know what, I'm going to bring all my friends in here (my entourage!) and pay or subsidise them so they can join me in this warped, airless place where you can buy what you want but no one ever tells you the truth.* I couldn't do that. My family and my friends knew the bubble themselves. Mum, Dad, Sarah, Alfie, Jess, Phoebe, Miquita, Danny – I could go on and on – their work or their upbringing or their experiences had allowed them to witness it up close to some degree, and not on my ticket. They were wise to it, most of them, and they weren't game. I'd tried being friends with people who'd already staked their place inside the bubble, and that certainly hadn't worked. That wasn't friendship, it was gameship, and I wasn't interested in it.

But it does help to explain why I found it so easy to lose my grip on reality and why I wasn't better at dismissing things like tabloid stories as the next day's fish-wrap. Everyone I knew, it seemed, worked in the media, and fame was currency for us all. We all dealt in it, and so it was hard to separate myself away from its lusty power.

That was one part of my problem. But the other was confusion, because one of the most marked side effects of fame, *wherever* you come from and *whoever* you are, is just that: utter, utter confusion. Fame, by its very nature, is confusing. It creates around you another persona, like a Ready Brek orange glow. Of course, the crowds of people who read about you or listen to your records only know a version of you that has been projected into the world, and it may not matter whether that version is a benign, perhaps more bland, perhaps more interesting version of who you are in real time, in the real world. But my problem was that the projected version of me – public Lily, the Lily in the media, the Lily most people saw or read about – became *so* distorted that even I had trouble reconciling her with the original cast from whence she came. In photographs she looked just like me. Sure, some of the lines and stories in the tabloids were pure, made-up falsehoods, but if public Lily was on TV or on the radio or writing on her blog, she was me – or at least a version of me. It was confusing. Who was in charge of who? Who was real? The quiet person who felt alone inside or the noisy one that everyone listened to, but who seemed unable to control what she was saying?

Let me explain this disparity, and how it happened, a bit more. I knew, once I'd been on the cover of *OMM*, that there was press interest in me. I knew journalists were talking about me in the Groucho Club, and that kind of thing. But it felt fine at that point. I talked about my music and how I wrote my blog, and that stuff was reported. The journalists added their impressions of me or what they thought of my songs and that was fine, too. Things were beginning to get crazy in terms of the amount of press that I was getting, but at least I could still recognise myself in what was being written. Sometimes people made a mistake or two about me, but they felt like simple errors or hurried research rather than any deliberate falsifying. Similarly, the way I was living wasn't a million miles away from the way I'd been living before my music began to take off.

Of course, before the summer of 2006, I wasn't performing on stage with a hit record, but in terms of my actual day-to-day life, things were recognisable and felt familiar. Crucially, I still felt safe. Yes, I was on tour doing the festival circuit with my own music, but I was with Tunde and the Future Cut boys who I'd been with in Manchester, and I'd known my assistant, Emily, for years because she was my sister Sarah's best friend. With us, too, was a roadie called Derek who was also in his own band called Peter and the Test Tube Babies, and a front-of-house guy called John Delph. We got on well. We were on the level. We were on the road together living out of a splitter van with a table in it and nine seats. Our rider consisted of tins of Strongbow cider and Monster Munch crisps, and we would sit and eat and chat. It wasn't starry or crazy and no one was paranoid or behaved badly. It was a right laugh. It was the best of times. I long for those kinds of times now.

But, even then, it wasn't quite as it seemed.

Not being able to trust everyone, even people I'd known for years, was just one of the rude lessons I had to learn that summer. Another was that my own words, even in a taped interview, could be taken out of context, and could affect what I'd said. For example, in the summer of 2006, just as I was hitting the big time, the journalist Alex Bilmes (now the editor of *Esquire*) came to my manager's office to interview me for a feature in *GQ*. We immediately hit it off, and over time have become good friends. But he was the first person to set me up in an interview. He goaded me, I said stuff, he laughed, and I said more stuff to make him laugh more. I wanted to impress him with my irreverence and ballsy wit. Alex didn't misquote me, but because he wrote himself out of the piece, it read as if I was slagging off Madonna, say, out of the blue, just for the hell of it.

So, he'd ask, 'What do you think of Madonna?'

I'd reply, 'She might have meant something once, but I don't know anyone my age who cares.'

But the piece would read as if I'd just spouted off about Madonna and her irrelevance without being asked specifically about her.

Basically, it doesn't matter how a journalist gets their copy, as long as they're not making something up, and what you've said is on record. There's no point feeling hard done by. Instead, you learn that all that matters – for the little life of that little piece over which *they* have total control – is what you've said. You learn not to say stuff or how to say it more carefully. You learn to be more guarded. It took me a long time to learn these lessons.

I didn't feel taken advantage of by Alex and his article or that kind of press. I thought it was fair game. I felt like I was learning the ropes. I thought: *OK, here's where you wise up. Slag off Madonna and you run into her huge fan base on the internet going mental at you. Fair play to them.*

Often, I was called out on things I'd said. Quite right, too. When I was writing my blog on Myspace, before I was famous, it felt like I was writing for myself. I knew people were reading the blog, but it felt like a safe and intimate forum. I didn't feel self-conscious when I wrote, and I didn't have any particular agenda.

A typical entry went like this: 'Rudely awoken by the radio and that trollop Edith Bowman warbling on about how she is just BESTEST friends with just about anyone, so long as they are in a band and preferably wearing skinny jeans and stripy cardigans, and how the Magic Numbers are just absolutely brilliant, AGAIN.'

Edith Bowman had read what I'd written. When I met her, she asked me why I had called her a trollop. I was upfront about it. 'I'm sorry,' I said. 'You always came across to me as this square person who has all these musician friends. Plus, I was cross with you because I was desperate for you to play one of my records on your show. But you're right. I didn't know you. I'm really sorry.'

Edith Bowman was cool about it when I apologised. She's a cool person.

Alfie, on the other hand, hasn't forgiven me for writing a song about him: 'Alfie'. He hates it and still resents me for writing it. I don't blame him. When I wrote it, it didn't occur to me that it would be a hit or that big-time fame was around the corner. Even though I was, by then, writing with Greg in a studio in LA, there wasn't an audience waiting to hear what I'd written. There was no outside noise coming into the studio. I was just doing my thing, writing songs about what I knew.

But Alfie *still* gets asked about it in interviews. That's tedious for him. I know how he feels, because when I first started doing well, all anyone wanted to talk to me about was my dad. That's the way the fame bubble rolls. I got famous and my dad was also kind of famous, ergo he must have passed on that fame to me, so even though this piece is about you, let's talk about him and how really you cheated a little bit, getting into the club, right, Lily Allen? Correct? It's as if I had joined the family firm — *The Allens: our business is fame!* — without earning my own stripes. That's what got to me: this assumption that I had it easy, that I just snuck in the door.

All this was a steep learning curve, and not all of it was pleasant, but at least I could still detect myself in what I was reading or seeing or hearing. Yep, they'd got things a bit wrong; or, shit, I should have thought for longer before I spoke; or, fuck, better not to get drunk with journalists. Lessons in the fame game, all.

What wasn't a lesson but a violation was what happened with the tabloid press. That was a whole other experience, and it was deeply confusing. It made me mad, and I don't say that lightly.

It began in July 2006, after my first single, 'Smile', was released. It started climbing the charts immediately, and by the middle of the month, it hit number one, knocking Shakira's 'Hips Don't Lie' off the top spot.

The weekend before that, I'd been at the festival T in the Park. There was a guy there from *NME*, who asked to interview me. I agreed.

'How are you going to celebrate?' he asked, a twinkle in his eye.

'Oh, you know,' I said, sarcastically, all pseudo-sophistication, 'probably get loads of cocaine in.' I was twenty-one years old, hanging out at a festival, and I liked the guy. I thought we were flirting.

That was on a Saturday. The next morning the front cover of *News of the World* was taken up by a photograph of me, along with a headline like: 'Number One Star goes on Coke Bender'.

And so it began.

Sure, I took drugs, but a coke bender? What coke bender? I was confused. It was that moment, when the bubble of unreality was blown up big, and I found myself floating around – no boundaries, no right way up, no smooth ground, no anchor to the earth – it was then that Cartoon Lily was born.

Looking back, I think I was traumatised by this first headline. Certainly, I felt overwhelmed, especially because once this relationship with the tabloids started, I didn't seem able to stop it. I'd do or say one thing, whether good or bad, and the tabloids would write whatever they wanted, create whatever story they had decided to run in order to perpetuate whatever narrative they'd decided to create.

Sometimes tabloid stories about you are totally false. Mostly, they contain some kernel of truth – you were in a certain place at a certain time – but they then veer very far away from any actual truth. You are photographed crying, ergo it's because you are having a mental breakdown. You went to a boarding school for a bit and your parents have done well for themselves: that explains your success.

You are watched joshing with Elton John at an awards ceremony: you started a catfight and you've offended a National Treasure. You're photographed not wearing your wedding ring: your marriage must be over. You're never seen with your kids: you're a terrible mother. And so on.

Sometimes, it's easy to dismiss these narratives. Yes, I was photographed being sick at Notting Hill Carnival in the summer of 2016. Yes, I had a whitey. No, I wasn't losing my shit. At other times, worryingly, they can start to become self-perpetuating. It's an insidious process. 'How *are* you?' people you know ask, all concern, after reading about, say, your apparent marital problems. 'I'm fine,' you reply, upbeat.

'No,' they go on, however well-meaning or eager for gossip. 'How are you *really*?'

Oh God, you think. *How* are *things really? I thought they were fine. Maybe they're not. Maybe it isn't all fine after all.*

Of course, if you're totally strong and stable, you can dismiss all this noise. If you come from a secure, grounded background, and you've got a great support system in place, then fame may well be a breeze. I wouldn't know.

And there are the positives, of course. Here's the other thing that happened when 'Smile' came out: I was given the most amazing amount of affirmation from people, and that was both confidence-building and brilliant for my self-esteem. I was sent clothes and shoes, and was being dressed by the best fashion houses. But it all added to the roller coaster: one minute I was, like, *This is incredible.* But then I'd wake up and see the newspapers and it was, *Bang! Back down the other side…* If it was positive, it was lovely, but if it was negative – and it was mostly negative – it was hideous and baffling.

It is also isolating in all kinds of ways. The most obvious is to do with trust.

Sometimes the tabloids don't make up stories at all. They buy them. The first time this happened to me was also soon after 'Smile' came out. The song was about Lester, and I was honest about that in interviews. I would be asked: 'Who is the song about?' And I'd reply: 'My first proper boyfriend who I was very much in love with.' Every time I said that, I thought back to that heartbreaking phone call from Lester on his sail boat when he told me that he was no longer interested in me.

But Lester did, in fact, become interested in me once more – when 'Smile' hit number one. At least, he became interested in what he could make by selling his version of our relationship to the *News of the World*. The story was all: 'Our mad sex romps in the forest high on E,' and he was apparently paid £80,000 for it. It's true, we did have sex outside, at his cousin's party. She was rich and, like Lester, upper class, and the party was at her estate in Ireland. There were plenty of private places there to have sex on a warm night with your boyfriend of two years. It didn't feel salacious or wild when we were doing it. My memory of it had been that it was sweet and intimate and private.

But the worst part about Lester selling his story wasn't that he did it, it was that none of his friends – who had been my friends too, or so I'd assumed, said anything about it at all. It seemed that betraying someone you loved for money was apparently fine. I found that confusing.

At least with that story, I knew it was Lester who sold it. But the worst part about people being paid to leak stories about you isn't that they do it (who am I to judge? Who knows what dire financial situation they might be in?), it's the not knowing *who* is doing it.

All sorts of things go through your mind. You think, *Is it my cousin's mate?* Who fucking knows? And if you've already got abandonment issues, which I do, then it becomes quite worrisome and isolating. You become paranoid. You don't know who to trust. You don't know if you can trust *anyone*.

You can see that things become confusing – even in your real life, with people that you really know. It's even more confusing trying to keep track of the persona that has been created: which bits were drawn by you, and which bits were add-ons or creations by the tabloids.

I got lost in fame sometimes, but I never pursued it for its own sake, or tried to preserve it. What I wanted was to find my voice, and find my voice I did. But just as this miraculous process was happening and as I began to realise I could write songs, I felt like my newly forming foundations were snatched out from under me, and that my voice was no longer my own. That's what that headline in the *News of the World* did. It twisted my words into lies. That's a big deal when your currency is based on telling the truth. I don't just mean to the outside world, but for myself, too. For me, writing a song and then performing it to people requires a huge confidence trick, and that trick was based not on technique or a learned skill, but on wanting to express myself – my real, true self.

That's why I found tabloid fame so devastating. I'd struggled for years before becoming a singer, but that struggle wasn't to achieve outside recognition. I wasn't even struggling in a bid to master my craft, or any craft. I was struggling with *myself*. I was struggling with getting out from under the shadow of my childhood and feeling so invisible and meaningless for so many years. My struggle was to feel like I existed as a human fucking being. Then, after finding Lester and feeling loved (ta dah!), I struggled with being dumped, with losing love and with feeling like I had lost my future. Fame and success? I was, like, *Whatevs. It's oxygen I'm after here, a fucking lifeline.*

That's why it was so devastating to read that headline.

And why it was so confusing to have to think, *I said that?*

I was, like, *But I didn't say that.*

I was, like, *I've just found my voice but* that *isn't my voice.*

Part of me was, like, *Oh shit, I need to shut this shit down.* But I couldn't. And I didn't want to, either. I am opinionated and I wanted to speak my mind. I felt confused and bewildered and like part of me was being eaten alive, but I didn't want to shut up, or to let the tabloids beat me.

Also, the messages I was getting were, empirically, mixed. Sometimes it was positive: 'It's so great to have someone not scared of talking,' people said. 'Pop has been sterile for so long. You're so refreshing.'

'Come and be in our gang,' other famous people said. 'Please be on our TV show,' they asked. 'Come and be funny on *Never Mind the Buzzcocks* or *The Friday Night Project* or whatever. Come and take the piss out of yourself and join us lot over here. We're clever and knowing, and we've pulled off the trick of getting the fame bubble to remunerate and reward us, even while we pretend we're deflating it. We're all in this together, us famous ironical lot.'

More often, or so it felt, it was negative. 'You're a disgrace,' Lorraine Kelly said, wringing her hands and slagging me off on national TV. 'You're a fraud,' said Julie Burchill in the *Daily Mail*. 'You're nothing but a middle-class poser.'

It was exhausting. Nothing I was saying was particularly controversial or out of the ordinary. But I was a young woman in an industry that preferred its females compliant and subservient, hungry – and preferably a bit cold and shivery on account of not wearing enough clothes. Vulnerable, in other words, and therefore more pliable and easier to get in line, that line being that what sells is youth, sex appeal and a lean bod, with no unsightly flabby female bits: not of body and not of mind.

I wanted to rail against all that, but I was also a needy young adult learning how to process everything I was learning. I insisted on not being objectified, and yet, oh God, I minded that I wasn't being objectified enough. I hated that young female singers were being reduced to objects of desire, and yet I longed to be intensely desired myself. I was twenty-one years old with not much experience under my belt. I was messy, needy, narcissistic, fearful. I was outraged, outspoken, fearless. I was defensive one minute, didn't give a shit the next.

My way of dealing with all these contradictory feelings and the huge confusion I felt—? I waved it all away with drink and alcohol and sex and shopping and attaching myself to men. Sometimes, I binged on drugs or drink or food to get a feeling of blindness between myself and the world I was now inhabiting, and sometimes I whittled myself away, because being thin and streamlined made me less: less messy and less of a grotesque cartoon character.

You may remember Cartoon Lily from those tabloid years, over a decade ago. She hung around for years, and still surprises me by making the odd appearance in the press even now. Cartoon Lily was successful in terms of her career, but she was a mess as a person. She took too many drugs, got drunk, didn't mind her manners, said what she thought, didn't watch her back, and was loose with money and sex. Her weight fluctuated. Her hair changed colour. She wasn't bad-looking and she could clean up all right, but you could get photos of her looking rough as shit. She was a tabloid editor's dream.

I'd see her in the tabloids – she was me, apparently – talking at a party or stumbling home a bit drunk and I'd read about how revolting she was and I'd think: *Really? That cartoon girl is me?* Or, *No, not really?* Because quite often it's hard to know what is actually going on or what really matters. For example: *You're publishing photographs of my vagina in a newspaper? For real?* But it's not really real, because it's a photograph in a newspaper, and if you were with me in real life you probably wouldn't have seen my vagina at all. It's not like I got it out. It is only after the event and via a digital image, created with flash photography and a semi-sheer dress, that I'm exposed.

So, on the one hand, I've got a vagina and there are lots of cameras in my life so that happens and it's not that important in the scheme of things, but on the other, it's disorientating, because it's hurtful when someone tells you to put your minge away in a national newspaper. But you've got to train yourself not to feel hurt, because actually, in terms of fame and the tabloid press, that kind of thing is the least of it.

If you become famous quickly, it's new terrain. You don't know where the pitfalls are, so you have to learn the lie of the land as you stumble along. I stumbled a lot and fell into all kinds of traps.

I think that's partly why I was never reverent with journalists. Many of them, it seemed to me, had their own agenda and were going to write the narrative they already had in their head, no matter what I said. More dangerous still, sometimes the way they manipulated situations (paying people to leak stories, making stuff up, following me or intimidating me until I snapped) to suit their narrative (that I was gross, gobby Cartoon Lily, always getting myself into trouble) made me change my actual behaviour. It's one thing when the tabloids warp your reality, but it becomes something more dangerous and worrying when their stories start to affect your reality.

This happened to me most notably in 2007, when I was going out with Ed Simons, from The Chemical Brothers. He's an actual human person too, and he's now training to be a psychiatrist, but in terms of the tabloids we didn't exist as human beings, with rights to privacy and dignity: we were pop stars and therefore fair game. When I started seeing Ed

I was working hard writing my second album, *It's Not Me, It's You*, and my career was in full swing. Then, not long after Ed and I had got together, the tabloids called my press agent to seek confirmation that I was pregnant. I wasn't, but even though my press agent firmly denied it, the news editor of *The Sun*, a guy called Chris Pharo, was adamant that his paper was going to run a story saying I was.

I was dumbfounded. Why would *The Sun* think I was pregnant? Even if they'd been going through my bins they couldn't have found a pregnancy test because I hadn't done one. Maybe someone followed me to the gynaecologist, maybe they knew (somehow) that I'd had my coil removed at around this time. I'd had it removed not because I wanted to conceive, but because I'd had it in for five years, and it was time to give my body a break and use another method of contraception.

It didn't really matter why or how *The Sun* had a pregnancy theory in their heads (maybe they were just bluffing to get any reaction out of me); what was important from my point of view was that it didn't hit the headlines. My Catholic nan was very ill at the time – she died months later – and the idea that a dying woman would have to read something untrue that would upset her gravely seemed unbearable to me. I had to stop it.

I wrote Chris Pharo a measured email. I figured that being polite would help not stir the pot. I told him that my grandmother was very ill, and that she wouldn't survive reading something like this in a newspaper. 'Please don't write the story,' I said.

Then, a week or so passed and I missed my period.

I was, in fact, pregnant, and freaked out on many levels.

How on earth did *The Sun* find out I was pregnant before I did? This is insane, I thought. My paranoia went into overdrive. If *The Sun* knows I'm pregnant, and I don't announce it, they'll be on the prowl for an abortion story. I was literally traumatised by the 'coke bender' front-page story a year or so earlier, so I didn't know how I would cope with this. The shock, combined with hormones, being followed everywhere I went by several men on bikes with cameras, and generally feeling hunted, resulted in me being completely crippled with anxiety. I was even more scared because I had sent an email directly to Chris Pharo from my personal email, denying being pregnant. I thought that they might make trouble for me if, say, the *Mirror* got hold of the news and printed it first.

I didn't know what to do. I hadn't meant to get pregnant and I knew I didn't want to have the baby. But now, I'd have to get the pregnancy terminated in the public eye and under the spotlight of the tabloid press, all the while enduring their hypocritical moralising. That seemed an appalling prospect. I also worried that Ed, who was a successful guy in his forties (a good partner, in other words), might think that I'd got pregnant accidentally on purpose, as a way to trap him. I also worried, on the other hand, that if I told Ed I didn't want the baby then that would be akin to declaring our relationship futureless and thus risk him leaving me. And this was me, Lily, we're talking about: I'd do anything not to actively risk a guy leaving me.

So that night I had to tell Ed that I was pregnant and I had to pretend to be happy about it. Then I had to tell the world that I was pregnant. And pretend to be happy about it. And then, three weeks later, I had to fake a miscarriage. It felt to me like the only way to explain my pregnancy and it ending with some kind of dignity. I was 24 years old and five weeks pregnant, with raging hormones. I felt like I was a bad person because I was demanding huge amounts of attention for announcing my pregnancy to the world, early, pretending to be happy about it, and then pretending to be distraught at having had a miscarriage. (Ed and I broke up a few months later, anyway – not surprisingly, given my dysfunction.)

The tabloids kept telling me that I was out of control, that I was drinking too much and taking too many drugs and so I began to think: yeah, that's me. I was young. I couldn't talk to anyone about the truth. I felt like I was serving a sentence, and that sentence was: *You can't talk to anyone. You can't trust anyone. You're alone.*

I served that sentence for many years and paid highly for my feelings of distrust and paranoia. As I went forward, I tried to paper over feeling isolated in all kinds of ways: by attaching myself too quickly to men (how could I be alone if I'd found a partner?) and by paying too much attention to what floated around me, on the surface: how good I looked (or didn't), the clothes I could buy or acquire, the parties I could go to, the success I could earn, the fun I could have (it wasn't all bad), the drink I could consume, and the drugs I could score and take. Instead of cleaning myself up and proving them wrong or just plain ignoring them completely (which I found impossible), I reacted to their constant haranguing by taking a lot of drugs.

Reader, I scored and took a lot of drugs.

GLASTONBURY

I started taking drugs recreationally when I was fifteen. My friends and I went to squat parties every weekend to listen to drum and bass and jungle music, and there was quite a lot of ketamine around. We took that because it was cheap. Coke back then was something that older boys gave you if you were young and pretty. We couldn't afford to buy it ourselves. But what we were really after was ecstasy.

I discovered the joys of E at Glastonbury. Glastonbury has always been part of my life, and drugs, for me, have always been part of Glastonbury. That's why I haven't been there recently. I no longer want to go somewhere for three days and take lots of drugs, but I'd find it difficult to go there and *not* take drugs. It's a shame. I know people who do go there sober, and have a great time, and there are NA meetings at Glastonbury these days. But I'm not there yet. I'm still, like, *Why do it to yourself?* For me, being with half a million people high on drugs while I'm sober would be an act of masochism.

I know my limits. I can't do it.

The first time I went to Glastonbury was in 1985. I was eight weeks old. For us Allens, Glastonbury was more important than Christmas, and certainly it was when more of our family gathered together. But even though it was a family thing, us kids had our own identities at the festival, because we had our own friends down there within the larger group and we could go off, in our little groups, and find the music we wanted to listen to or the tents we wanted to dance in or the food we wanted to eat, and that felt like a rare thing. I think that's why I liked it so much. We could be independent and find what we liked on our own, but there was this big family unit built around the campfire that was always there for us to return to.

It wasn't all idyllic. Glastonbury isn't May Day. The grown-ups took drugs, sometimes too many. As I got older, I began to recognise other people's drug-related anxiety. You know how the mood can shift at 4am when people are off it? When things get sketchy? When things stop being funny and people stop sharing drugs and start to go off to the bathroom alone or with just one chosen person and the atmosphere turns sour and aggressive rather than fun and communal? I learned to recognise that moment when I was a child. I think that's why I always stop now when the atmosphere changes. It's a no-go zone for me. I've hammered away at drugs and drink, and, as you'll see later, I did hit a rock-bottom point with drink, but until that moment, I was never someone who kept going after a party turns dark. I can recognise it instantly, I'm sure, because I witnessed it at Glastonbury with my dad and his mates around the campfire. My reaction is flight. I take myself off, quickly, quietly, wherever I am, and either leave, or if the party is at my house, put myself to bed, even if it means taking sleeping pills or downers to get to sleep.

But before things turn sour with drugs, taking them can be brilliant. I loved my first ecstasy experience. I was fifteen, and I did it with Miquita and Phoebe. I think we had twenty quid between us, so we scored three Es, took one each, then somehow got separated. It can be frightening to be at a festival alone and high on drugs, especially if it's your first time on ecstasy, but I was OK. One thing my dad had taught me at Glastonbury over the years was the art of the blag, and I managed to blag someone to take me to the drum and bass tent where I knew they'd be dancing, then I blagged the MC to make an announcement for them to meet me in the middle of the tent. It worked. But then, so much seems to go right at Glastonbury. Over the years we tried on everything there. Occasionally we got given backstage passes for certain gigs through Dad's friend, the musician Joe Strummer, but more often than not we had to talk and wangle our way to the side of the stage if we wanted to watch someone close up and be in on the action.

We didn't just blag stuff at Glastonbury as kids and teenagers, we stole it, too. We were terrors. We never had any cash there – even if my dad had money at that point (and it went up and down), he wouldn't give it to us, and certainly not at Glastonbury where he knew it would have been spent on drugs – so we used to nick it from the grown-ups. We stole other stuff, too. If it was a muddy year, we'd go around the jewellery shops and pinch rings and earrings by dropping them onto the mud on our boots, then walking away from the stall. We'd wash them clean, then sell them. You didn't get much for a bit of hippy silver, but you might score a couple of smoothies or a flag or whatever else we were after back then.

Dad didn't pay us much attention, but it didn't seem to matter at Glastonbury. He was *there*. But, sometimes things went wrong. In 1998, he had a heart attack at Glastonbury. That was pretty intense. I was fourteen and I remember coming back to the campfire to find Joe's wife, Lucinda, waiting for me. She told me that Dad had been taken to the field hospital in an ambulance and that I should go and see him.

They've got an A&E section at the festival, and when I got there I felt reassured, because there was Dad, all propped up neat and tidy in a hospital bed, hooked up to various tubes and machines, looking relatively OK.

The heart attack was presumably the result of him taking too much cocaine.

Next door to Dad was a girl who'd lost it on acid. She came over and knelt down in front of me. 'Have you seen Dave?' she said.

'No,' I replied.

'I've lost my boyfriend,' she went on, a faraway look in her eyes. 'He's called Dave, but I don't know where he is. Can you help me find him?'

'OK,' I said. 'What does he look like?'

She held her fingers up an inch apart. 'He's *this* big,' she said, squinting her eyes as if measuring him up. 'With brown hair.'

I remember thinking, *I'm not the adult in this situation, but I'm going to assume that role and try and reassure this girl.*

'Dave is going to turn up,' I told her. 'He just might be a bit bigger than you're expecting.'

Dad was discharged from the hospital tent the next day. He got taken back to our campsite and tucked up in bed in one of the caravans there. I went to check on him, and found him with a rolled-up bank note in his hand and a book on his lap, about to snort a line of cocaine from it. I was furious. 'You've just had a heart attack from taking too much cocaine and now *you're taking cocaine?*' I shouted.

He didn't care. He took the coke anyway.

Glastonbury stopped being a family thing after Joe died in 2002. Dad still went after that, but it was different. I started to go with Miquita and Phoebe instead of Dad. And when I was with Lester I went with him. After Joe died, the Eavises carved out a section of the site and called it Strummerville, and every year we were given a special spot there.

That's what made performing at Glastonbury even more special. I have this real connection to the place, so playing there was this insanely amazing thing for me. I did my first gig at Glastonbury in 2007. I was on the Pyramid Stage. Being given that stage felt like I'd gone straight to the top. It felt magic. It felt amazing. I'd spent years blagging at Glastonbury, after all, and it had always been a big achievement just to wrangle a backstage wristband. And so, at twenty-two years old, to get given a block of fifty passes to hand out myself, because this time I *am* the band? That felt fucking nuts. One of the things about playing a festival is that there is so much else going on. Some people want to see you play, but they haven't made it over to your stage yet. When you start playing, you see people rushing over. What feels like an empty field suddenly starts filling up from all four corners. That's an amazing thing to watch, and it makes you feel great. Sometimes, though, the field doesn't fill up at all.

At Glastonbury the field has always filled up for me, but there have been festivals that I've done when it hasn't, and that's been awful. Performers call it 'the fear of the festival', because you've got to win people over, even the people right up close to the stage in the front rows – especially those people, in fact. Chances are they've come to see whoever is headlining the festival, not you, and they're just waiting out your set to keep their hard-won spot. If you can win those people over and gather a festival crowd together, you feel like you can do pretty much anything.

Sometimes, failing to connect, even if it's with just one person, can make a difference to a gig, and make you feel like you've done a dud show. In 2007, when I played the Pyramid Stage at Glastonbury, I also did an impromptu show on the Friday night to launch the Park stage. It was the first time Emily Eavis had her own section of the festival to plan and run. Emily asked me to play the Park at the last minute to replace the singer M.I.A., who had cancelled on Emily with only hours to go.

It wasn't a good experience, mainly because there was a girl at the front who was clearly livid that M.I.A. was not going to appear. I can still see her face now, and her look of outrage when she saw it was me up on stage instead of M.I.A. She shouted abuse directly at me the whole way through the gig. The Park stage is relatively small, and you feel close to the audience, which is a good thing. But it meant that the girl's reaction and anger threw me. I understood what she was saying and I agreed with her. I didn't think I was as cool as M.I.A. either.

Most of the time, for all my bluster, I didn't think I was cool at all. That's why I got so defensive when I was slagged off in public. Of course, I should have laughed it all off, and these days I do. But back when I was in the thick of all the fame and confusion and felt at home only really when I had a bundle of dramas under my arm, I found it impossible not to take it all too seriously.

CELEBRITY

Gordon Ramsay: 'What do you think of Lily Allen? Chick with a dick?'

Cheryl Cole: Nods. Laughs. Nods again.

Oh my fucking God! Cheryl Cole basically called me a chick with a dick on national fucking television.

When 'Smile' was released as a single, one of the B-sides was a song called 'Cheryl Tweedy'. It's a jaunty little number about my own self-loathing. The first verse goes: 'I wish I had qualities like / Sympathy / Fidelity / Sobriety / Sincerity / Humility. Instead I got lunacy.' The chorus goes like this: 'I wish my life was a little less seedy / Why am I always so greedy? / Wish I looked just like Cheryl Tweedy.'

Cheryl Cole, née Tweedy, was still a pop star in the fantastically popular band Girls Aloud back then. She was petite and perfectly formed, a dinky, perfect pop princess who always looked great. Meanwhile, I often felt like a mess. She talked about my song in an interview. She said she was kind of honoured by it, but managed to be a bit dismissive about it at the same time.

I wasn't having that.

I responded by writing on my Myspace blog: 'Cheryl, I don't really want to look like you. I was being ironic. Nobody *really* wants to look like you, they just think they do.'

A few months later in May 2007, Cheryl and her bandmate Kimberley Walsh appeared on a Gordon Ramsay TV show called *The F Word*. The format of the show entailed famous people eating in a mocked-up restaurant while Ramsay went round the tables in his chef's whites, telling them off for not liking his food enough, and gossiping about other celebs. 'What do you think of Lily Allen?' Ramsay asked Cheryl, after discovering she hadn't eaten her foie gras. 'Chick with a dick?' he asked, egging her on. She laughed when he said that. It clearly tickled her. 'Chick with a dick,' she responded, nodding her head and laughing some more.

That's when things turned sour. 'Cheryl,' I wrote on my blog, 'if you're reading this, I may not be as pretty as you but at least I write and SING my own songs without the aid of Auto-Tune... I must say, taking your clothes off, doing sexy dancing and marrying a rich footballer must be very gratifying for you, your mother must be so proud, stupid bitch.'

Imagine writing that. It was such a horrible thing to say. Of course Cheryl's mum was proud of her. Why wouldn't she be?

It was ridiculous. I bitched at Cheryl because she insulted

me after I provoked her. You can see how it can go, this playground game. The crazy part was that we then had this feud, as if the hatred between us was a real thing. We didn't *know* each other. When all this happened, I'd never *met* Cheryl Cole. I did resent Girls Aloud's success back then, though. There was me, in the left corner, all self-proclaimed feminism, defiant in my prom dresses and trainers, proud of writing my own songs and speaking my own mind. And in the right corner, as I saw it, were Girls Aloud and their ilk, colluding with the oppressors and perpetuating what we were all up against by wearing skimpy clothes and singing songs written by other people. I was the liberated one, OK? I was righteous. I was calling it out.

What a joke. Now, I realise, it's all a lot more complicated. Now, mostly I think: *Why judge people like that?* And, anyway, me liberated back then? Hardly. I wore prom dresses because I hated my legs and I wanted to cover them up. Liberated? I was jealous. I was frustrated. I was struggling with my own issues around sexuality. I'd never even had an orgasm. And then here were these gorgeous girls – my peers, colleagues so to speak, and co-workers – taking their clothes off with wild abandon and being loved and rewarded for it. I couldn't take it. Sorry, Cheryl. I was angry because I hadn't come yet.

I think Cheryl Cole took what I said to heart. I assumed she'd come back at me and that our fight would continue and that everyone in the entire country read *The Sun* and would be following our feud. That's how famous I felt in 2007.

★ ★ ★

When you're famous you get asked to do things you're not qualified for. For example, I've never had ambitions to act, but when I was famous I'd be sent scripts to read and parts to consider. I was asked to take the *lead* role in Neil LaBute's stage play *Fat Pig*, for example. How could I do that when I've never acted and had zero training? It must drive proper actors mad. Mostly, I just turned those kinds of things down. But then there are the things you do because they are on the fringes of your industry. Television presenting, for example.

Strictly speaking, then, I knew what I was doing when I was asked to present the GQ Awards in September 2008. I'd done plenty of TV by then and knew how to keep my shit together. But, boy, it's a long evening to get through. That year GQ had teamed up with Elton John's AIDS Foundation for the awards. Elton would host the evening, GQ would benefit from the publicity he generated, and money would be raised for the foundation. (Basically, at least while collectively wanking off, cash was being raised for a good cause.)

Elton asked me if I'd like to co-host the evening with him. I said I'd be delighted. Elton and I knew each other pretty well back then. His company, Rocket, was managing me. We were used to ribbing each other.

I drank throughout the ceremony: it was a GQ party with a lot of free champagne; drinking a lot is what everyone does. I got a bit slurry, bit messy. I was high. Everyone knew. No one cared, least of all Elton.

'Now we reach a very special point in the evening,' I said, reading from the autocue, when we came to introduce one of the final awards.

'What?' Elton ad-libbed. 'Are you going to have another drink?'

'Fuck off, Elton,' I said, and I meant it. 'I'm forty years younger than you. I've got my whole life ahead of me.'

Not one to be outdone, Elton turned to me and said, 'I can still snort you under the table.' He enunciated each word with crisp precision.

'I don't know what you're talking about,' I said. Even drunk, I knew not to kick this gambit around. The room was filled with journalists; we were being filmed. 'We don't usually do this...' I started, trying to get back on course.

Elton began to interrupt me again.

'Fuck off, Elton, actually,' I spoke loudly over him. 'Seriously.'

'All right,' he said, suddenly defensive, and we went back to script.

It was funny. The audience laughed. We were taking the piss out of each other. It was no big deal.

The next day, it was reported that we'd 'fallen out spectacularly' in a 'public cat fight', which marked the opening chapter of a 'feud'. We 'came to blows', the tabloids said, embarking on a 'scathing war of words'. It was obviously all my fault. I had appeared 'drunk and dishevelled', and my behaviour had been 'disgraceful'.

What a load of bollocks. Even Elton had to wade in and comment on the press' reaction. 'That was just such nonsense,' he said in an interview. 'We had a great time... I love Lily. She was feeling no pain, I was feeling no pain. I was sober, she wasn't, but it doesn't matter... We certainly didn't have a fall-out on stage.'

It's disconcerting when what is reported outside the bubble is different to what has gone on inside it. I got drunk at an awards party and bantered on stage with my co-host. We were photographed together with our arms around each other. NO! The papers said. You're a cat-fighting, drunken disgrace and now you're feuding with Sir Elton John.

That's the sort of thing that happens inside the fame bubble and its freak show hall of mirrors, and almost as soon as I was inside it, I knew I wanted out. I knew I wanted a real life with babies and a home and a life partner and, more and more, I realised I wanted it soon.

I'd already met Sam, the man I would marry, and a month later I would clean myself up and move in with him. He, I thought, would help provide me with my escape route.

It turned out to be easier than that. It turned out that once I stopped drinking and drugging and had a clear head, all I had to do was step away from the fame bubble and off it floated, without me. It turned out that my second album title was just as prescient as I'd hoped.

It's Not Me, Fame, you fucker, it turns out, *It's You*.

WORK,
PART TWO

You'd think that I might have felt self-conscious or under pressure when it came to making my second album. Making a follow-up album is famously a nightmare for a lot of recording artists if they've had a successful debut. They feel paralysed by self-doubt or crippled by high expectations. They've most likely been living in the fame bubble too, if their first album was a success. It's hard to write about success and fame in a song without sounding like a dick and quite often that's the only material you've got: being famous and riding the wave is all you've been doing.

Sure, there are moments of glamour: the parties and booze, and you can get laid any time. Drugs are plentiful, flowers arrive frequently, money slops about, freebies are dispatched, and you are welcomed into any party. Some people revel in all that. Others despise it. Most people jog along somewhere in the middle, trying to find a way to manipulate it so that they can enjoy both success and some kind of private and meaningful life. But however you feel towards it all – success and fame – it's not necessarily all that interesting in terms of creative material. I remember people talking to me and laughing about it. 'You did it once,' they'd say, about finding success with my first album. 'Good luck following it up!' *Yeah, thanks!* I would think. *How hilarious. Wouldn't it be funny if I lost it all!*

That didn't happen. My second record came easily. I'd been on the road for a year and a half before I got into the studio, and the songs seemed to come out all at once. I'm not sure that young artists today suffer from second-album syndrome in the same way as past generations, now that streaming has replaced traditional record buying and 'the album' has lost its totemic significance. I was on the cusp of that change. And, in fact, the experience of fame did prove a rich seam to mine. The dislocation between my inner and outer life, and the difference between how I felt and how I was portrayed in the press seemed so gaping that it warranted exploring. It was, for me, interesting and relevant material.

My first album, *Alright, Still* had been something of a patchwork, made up from a song here, a song there. I didn't want my second album to be like that. I wanted it to feel more streamlined, like one complete story. I also knew that the person I wanted to work with on it was Greg, and him alone. We already had a working shorthand, and he understood my references. I liked him, too. He's not showbizzy. I felt comfortable writing with him, and not self-conscious when working things out.

We started writing *It's Not Me* in a rented cottage in Moreton-in-Marsh in Gloucestershire in 2007. I wanted to get away from London, and I'd heard about these residential studios in the countryside that bands sometimes rent: private, mini Babington-type places with a recording suite next to the bar and a hot tub in the vegetable garden. I thought a stint somewhere like that would be fun and productive. But the label was, like, *Fuck off, we're not paying that much money for you to work.*

So I asked for a tiny cottage instead. It had a living room with a weird wall down the middle. I'd sit on one side and write on the sofa, and Greg would be on the other side, with his computer set up on the dinner table. We'd cross sides to play each other stuff. I'd sing riffs and verses or come up with a top line (the melody that drives a song), or I'd listen to the chords he was working on and be, like, 'Yep, that's good,' and the words would follow.

We had to have the curtains drawn all the time because a bunch of kids cottoned on to us being there, and they'd listen in, tapping away in time and trying to learn the lyrics I was banging out. You can hear them singing along on some of the early demos. But other than the kids, there weren't many distractions. We didn't have Wi-Fi and didn't miss it.

By the end of week one, we'd written three songs: 'Go Back to the Start', 'The Fear' and 'Who'd Have Known'. When I wrote 'Who'd Have Known', I thought, *OK, this one's a goer. What a great hook!* I never usually think that about my music. It was the same with 'The Fear', which became my first hit from my second album. I had no idea that I'd written what would become a seminal song for me. I write to tell a story and express myself; my lyrics are lodged in particular experiences and places rather than being deliberate anthems. I write songs, not hits. If a song is good, people will connect with it. You don't have to trick them into it.

Greg used to say that I write best when I'm upset, hungover, sleep-deprived or driving. He's right. It's because half my brain is occupied with something else and hasn't got the energy to be critical or hamper the creative bit. Generally, if something comes quickly and naturally to me, then it tends to be good. It may then go through a hugely complex process and become a task to finish and produce, but if it comes quickly at the start, that's generally a sign that I'm on to something. And that's what happened with 'Who'd Have Known'. Greg played a chord and my brain followed that chord with the chorus. It was effortless.

We played it to Parlophone when they came to visit us at the end of week one to see how we were doing. 'Yeah,' they said. 'Great song. Just one problem – it's number one already.' I'd unknowingly cribbed Take That's song 'Shine'. I must have heard it on the radio in the supermarket or out in the world of Moreton-in-Marsh, and it had ear-wormed its way into my head and then out again as the chorus of my song. There's a computer programme now that can tell you if the song you've written is a rip-off of someone else's, and how much you should change it to make it just different enough that you don't have to pay to use someone else's work. I don't like doing that. If a song sounds good, it sounds good. Don't change it for the sake of saving money, but instead pay the money to whoever wrote the original music you've riffed.

I ran into the Take That guys back in London once I'd finished the album and I told them about 'Who'd Have Known'.

'I just need to tell you that I've got a song on my new record that I've stolen from you,' I said.

'That's funny,' they said. You bet they laughed. They got a huge chunk of money from my song. Most of the publishing income for that song goes to them. That's the way it goes. They wrote the hook, they got the money.

★ ★ ★

I won three Ivor Novello awards for *It's Not Me, It's You*, in 2010. These are the only awards that mean anything to me. The Ivors aren't that well known outside the music business because they aren't televised, but they're the ones that really count in the industry. They're awarded for excellence in songwriting, and the panel is made up of songwriters, rather than record label heads or execs. Four years later, in 2014, I was on the judging panel myself, so I know how seriously it is taken. Everyone on the panel – a group of peers – listens to the music over and over again, then endlessly discusses each song and argues about lyrics and chord progressions.

I'm proud of those awards. 'The Fear' won two, one for Best Song Musically and Lyrically, the other for Most Performed Song. That year I also won the award for Best Songwriter.

'The Fear' is about feeling lost in a lot of ways, and, after winning the award, I felt found. I felt heard. It felt like my work had landed somewhere proper and with weight. Forget about that with other awards, at least in the music industry.

Sure, they enhance your commercial currency and that's something, but they are about money, not merit.

I did like getting the *GQ* award, Woman of the Year, even though I knew as I was collecting it what an absurdity it was. I liked everyone going, yes, clap, clap, you *are* the best woman, and me smiling in response and trotting up to collect it and thinking: *You're right, I am a woman and I am very good at being a woman.* You might as well enjoy that bit of theatre, even though you know it's all nonsense and you wouldn't have been given the award if you hadn't agreed to pose topless for their cover.

The BRIT awards aren't like that. They aren't fun in the same way at all. They are run by the parasitic side of the business: the money men, and they feel like a gigantic ego-fest. They stink of wastefulness. It's, like, 'Look at all the money we're spending to help already established acts sell even more records.' I'm not blameless in it. I've contributed to the charade of it all.

I opened the show in 2010. I was pleased to be asked – it's a straight-up ego boost. But mostly it made me feel anxious, and I hated my performance. I didn't have a great relationship with the BRITs anyway, because I'd felt slighted by them in 2007 when I was nominated for five awards with *Alright, Still* but won not one. That was the year Amy Winehouse won everything. I remember seeing her perform with Mark Ronson that year and thinking: *That's it then, it's the Amy show. She's going to scoop it all up.* And she deserved to win everything, too. I'm a huge fan of Amy's work and I liked her too, though I never knew her well. What I didn't like was the way the industry pitted us against each other. In the press it was all, 'Here's Amy, this talented, troubled genius, whereas Lily is *quite* talented, but not up there with Amy.' Why did we have to be compared like that? There were fifty-five other people in the charts, so why were they taking these two people, who were quite different musically, and comparing them – just because they were both women?

Still, in 2010, I agreed to perform. To make it extra hard to say no, they dangle hints that you're going to win something – so you'd better play ball. I remember being told that I was going to get Best Female Solo Artist. When I heard that I thought, *Fuck, I don't want to be best 'female'.* That's fine for GQ magazine, but a music award should be about my work. I wanted best album. (Florence + The Machine won it, and good for her, but her being a good recipient didn't make me want it less.) I sang 'The Fear', which is doubly ironic given that the song was written as a reaction against the very values that the BRITs embody. There I was, singing a satirical song about fame and money on a platform that is all about celebrating fame and money, and boy, for me to sing it, they certainly spent money.

You don't get to decide, or at least I didn't, how your set will go. *They* tell you their vision for your performance. *You're going to come in on a rocket, Lil, and the stage is going to be full of female dancers with prams and then loads more dancers, guys this time, are going to come dangling down from the ceiling not wearing trousers and looking like pricks in pink helmets. Yeah, Lil? You feeling it?*

What I remember was feeling uncomfortable. 'Really?' I said. 'We have to have all of that?' I thought: *What the fuck is this all about? Aren't us women performers enough? Why do we need to have all this other shit going on behind us?* Then they tell you it's going to be great and they've got the amazing choreographer, Bianca Li, to stage it, and she *is* amazing, and you think, *Still, though, I don't like it, I feel uncomfortable.* Then you think, *There is so much I do for work that I'm not comfortable with, and this isn't up there with the worst shit, so fine, I won't fight this battle. Put me on the fucking rocket. Send in the clowns.*

The point is, those awards are hollow. They're about what deals and negotiations are going on between the labels. It's their show. That's why you saw Skepta and Stormzy being nominated in 2017, but neither one winning a single prize. What do you mean they didn't win? Which other artist has had a bigger impact on the music industry over the last few years? No one! But that would be a waste of a prize or two as far as the big companies are concerned, because both those guys are independent rather than signed to any major record label.

Still, at least they don't have to take half their clothes off to perform on those kinds of shows. I don't think Stormzy has ever had to deal with a comment about his arse. I had proved myself as a songwriter with *It's Not Me, It's You*, and yet I was still expected to look as hot as possible. I know, I went along with it. I took my clothes off for photo shoots and I often performed on stage in little more than my underwear. I felt sexy with this record. I was slim and in shape and I felt like I'd begun to take possession of my own sexuality.

I emphasise the word 'begun'. Me and sex? That's a whole other chapter.

SEX,
PART ONE

The second single to be rolled out from my second album was 'It's Not Fair'. It's a song about shitty sex and I think it rang true for a lot of people. Everyone thought I'd written it about the art dealer, Jay Jopling, who I was seeing around that time, and it would make a better story if it had been about him, but it's not. It isn't about any one guy. It's about a whole load of them. Hell, I wish shitty sex had been about a one-off experience.

I'd never had an orgasm when I wrote that song, not a single one, not with someone else and not by myself. I didn't masturbate when I was young, or in my teens, or even for most of my twenties. It's hard for me to unravel why. Certainly, pleasing myself in any way was never high on my list of priorities, and so the idea of actively exploring a zone that was apparently dedicated to pleasure felt impossible. I didn't feel like I deserved it. If you've spent most of your childhood feeling invisible, then it feels odd to start paying too much attention to yourself when you're on your own. It feels foreign and not right, because it's the opposite of what you're used to.

Once I started having sex I didn't come either, and so I thought I was just someone who couldn't, who didn't. Not coming when it comes to sex with a guy is common, especially for young women, who are inclined to be undemanding in bed. It seems too bold an ask for many of us and, for some reason, too many of us collectively retreat into passivity. Instead of exploring what makes us come (good oral sex being the surest route), we just fake it. I'd spent years faking orgasms by the time I wrote 'It's Not Fair'. The song was about feeling like a vessel for male pleasure.

I was with Jay for three or four months at the beginning of 2009, just as *It's Not Me* was being released. It was a fling. He was someone I knew through my dad's friend, Damien Hirst. Jay was on one side of Damien's life, my dad on the other. Dad hated Jay. He thought he was a posh wanker. That's probably one reason why I fancied him: I knew it would piss off my dad. And he was an older guy and I liked that. I liked that he took me to parties and in January sent a private jet to fly me to St Bart's to stay with him on the yacht he'd rented. I liked, or thought I liked, that he was rich, posh, secure, charming, and that he liked buying me expensive presents. I thought that was akin to him taking care of me.

There were paparazzi photos of us together taken on that yacht that were published in the tabloids. That's how my dad found out I was seeing someone from his world. He texted

Jay when he saw those photographs. I knew because I saw Jay get the text. His face turned white when he read it.

'You wait, Jay,' my dad texted. 'You wait 'til Angelica is sixteen.' Angelica is Jay's daughter. She was eleven years old in January 2009. Jay's ex-wife, Sam Taylor-Johnson, also texted him when she saw the photos. 'What are you doing going out with that dwarf?' she wrote.

Our relationship fizzled out. I can't remember exactly how it ended. I don't think the newspaper articles and my dad's text and Sam calling me a dwarf helped. I am very short but it was mean of him to show me her text. I remember thinking, *I don't need to hear that your ex-wife called me a dwarf, thank you very much.*

I was still dating Jay when I landed a contract with Chanel, to model for one of their campaigns. I rang him as soon as I got the news. It was massively exciting for me. I thought he'd be excited, too. 'I hope you're getting enough money for it,' he said, dryly, immediately deflating me.

'But look!' co-dependent me wanted to shout. 'Never mind the money! It means they think I'm beautiful. They think I'm pretty. See? Don't you think I'm pretty, too? Don't you love me? Don't you want to marry me now? Can't you be the one I hitch my wagon to, because I know we're massively unsuited, but you're here, next to me, so you'll do. You can be *him*. You can be the one to look after me!'

That's what I did with all the guys I dated. I attached myself to them as firmly as I could, and as stickily as they'd allow. I'd convince myself that they were right for me and we were meant to be together, even if really we would have been better off as friends. Indeed, I've stayed friends with all my ex-boyfriends, which might prove my point. I was confused at the beginning of my sexual life about my own desire for other people. Often, if a guy fancied me, that was enough for both of us. My self-worth was low and so being fancied, which I translated as being wanted (and thus loved), felt intoxicating enough to agree to sex.

Of course, I now know that a guy wanting to fuck you is not the same as him wanting you. Quite often he'll fuck you even if he doesn't want you, just because he can. He'll fuck you if he fancies you and he'll fuck you if he doesn't. In fact, he'll fuck you while he's in the process of rejecting you. A guy will sometimes beg to fuck you, not because he wants to fuck you that badly but because knocking down the wall you've put up is a turn on for him. Or maybe it's not the act of conquest that turns him on, but in a twisted version of S&M, he likes feeling humiliated by your attempts at rejecting him. Or maybe he likes witnessing your humiliation. Who fucking knows. Guys fuck women for all kinds of reasons, which sometimes include a genuine desire for intimacy and to connect on whatever level, but often don't.

That's why the only important thing is to know what *you* want as a woman and a human and a sexual person. You may not get it, and you may be overridden, but knowing what you want and making sure you try and assert that, means that at least you *start* from a place of power and strength.

I had none of that power when I first started having sex. I didn't have it for many years. I didn't claim it or even really know about it. Many women don't. Instead, I gave myself away. I gave myself away, but men also took from me. They helped themselves to me (yes, I'm talking about fucking me) when they knew or should have known (they were old and experienced enough) that I was too young and too naïve and too pliant to say no. I know a great many women will know exactly what I am talking about. It happens all the time, and it's not rape and it's not quite assault, but it's not right and it shouldn't happen.

I lost my virginity to a guy called Fernando. I met him in Brazil on holiday with Dad and Alfie when I was fourteen. There was a teen bar at the hotel where we were staying, and that's where we met. Fernando was twenty, and I was flattered that he fancied me, so off I went, trailing after him when he suggested going back to his room. I can't remember the sex. Mostly, I remember waking up late the next morning in Fernando's room and feeling panicked. *Shit*, I thought, *Dad is going to wonder where I am*.

Dad had wondered. Not only was I missing, but I'd been wearing a blue top the previous night when I'd disappeared, and a similar one had been found on the beach earlier that morning. Boats were scouring the sea. A search party had been called. The police had arrived. I'd caused a commotion. Dad was furious.

The second time I had sex was no more nurturing. I'd been watching my dad play a celebrity charity football game with a television star. After the match, the TV star left his football gear in my dad's car, and I was dispatched to his hotel to return it. We arranged to meet in the bar there. He bought me a couple of drinks, then took me up to his room and had sex with me. I was fourteen. He was nineteen, but to me he seemed like someone from a different generation. Afterwards, I felt funny about it. I knew what had happened wasn't right and so I told a friend of my dad's about it and he told my dad. I think I wanted my dad to know. I wanted him to make things better. In my teenage head, I wanted Dad to explode with protective anger, and to find the TV guy and beat him up.

Instead, my dad turned it into a shtick with his friends. They made up elaborate schemes to blackmail the guy and they rehearsed how they'd call him up and put the shits up him. They may even have gone so far as to make a phone call. I don't know. I just know that my dad turned me having sex with this guy I hardly knew into a joke between him and his mates. That didn't make me feel good.

It wasn't a coincidence that my first sexual partners were older than me. Five years isn't much when you are both adults, but when one of you is a young teenager and the other has hit twenty-ish years old, it's a big difference. A lot of experience, especially in terms of sex, gets packed into those late teen years. I was infatuated with older men because I felt that if I could prove to someone older that I could be mature too, then I was grown-up myself. I didn't feel comfortable being a child (as I may have mentioned 800 times). Sleeping with older men was a way of trying to kickstart the next chapter of my life. I'm sure too that any shrink in the land would explain it as me trying to find a father figure, because my own has always absented himself from that role.

I didn't flirt with the boys I hung out with, who were mostly older than me, too. I was used to relentless lad behaviour from spending time with my dad and his mates when he took me to the football on a Saturday or to hang out at Groucho's until five in the morning, so I knew how to shoot the shit with guys, but sex was different. I also thought that an older guy would be better equipped to show me what the whole sex thing was about, because I found it so mysterious myself. I wasn't sexualised as a young person. My sister was always the sexy one when we were growing up. I wasn't like her – she looked older than her years, I looked younger, she was tall, I was short, she looked sophisticated, I didn't – so, I didn't try and compete with her, especially when it came to the opposite sex. She could have sex with anyone she wanted… but when she did, it didn't seem to empower her. To me it looked like guys used her for sex. I didn't want that to happen to me, and so I shied away from exploring it actively, either by myself or with boys close to my own age. And yet, of course, the same thing happened to me. Sex didn't empower me for years. Those older men I had sex with at the beginning had no interest in helping me explore or discover sex. They didn't give a shit about me or any of that. That's why I wish I had started out exploring sex with a peer, rather than it being something done to me. I wish, too, that I had insisted on better sex earlier on in my life, or, at least, fairer sex or funnier sex, more fun sex or sexier sex. But I didn't. Not enough of us do.

The relationship I'm in now is the first time, I think ever, when sex has been an important factor. That's telling right there.

I wasn't friends with Dan before I got together with him. I met him at the Notting Hill Carnival in August 2015, when I went up to him and asked him if he had a Rizla. I fancied him. 'I can do better than that,' he said, and opened up a glasses case that was full of pre-rolled joints.

I'm in my thirties now and I have regular orgasms. I make sure of that. If I get back from working in the studio and I've got twenty minutes before I have to pick up the kids from school, I think: *Brilliant, I can get the dinner on and I've still got time for a quick wank.* Now I know what happens when I come, but for years, when I was faking orgasms all the time, I didn't even know what my real 'coming' noise was. I just did that ahhing noise you see on TV and in films. The guys I was with seemed to buy it. 'Did you come?' they'd ask. 'Oh, yeah,' I'd say. 'Oh, yeah, baby, I came.'

Still, even though I wasn't coming in my twenties, I was having plenty of sex. It wasn't all bad. Some of it, when I was with Lester and then Seb and then Ed, was loving and intimate, if not orgasmic. Other times, when I was single and out and about, it could be exciting. If I didn't get off at the end of sex, the beginning bit – the chase, the seduction – I found intoxicating.

In 2004, when I was nineteen, I had a crush on Mike Skinner from The Streets. Most teenagers, when they have a crush on a singer or a movie star, stick posters on their walls. Some wait around outside hotels or queue for hours to get close to the stage at concerts. If you're really determined you might try and become a groupie – but you need to be gorgeous and exotic with sex tricks up your sleeve to get that gig, and super-tough to survive it.

I wasn't going to settle for a homemade bedroom shrine or going to a few gigs, but I also knew that in a festival packed with girls in England, Mike Skinner from The Streets would never notice me.

But in Japan? *Maybe in Japan*, I thought, *where Skinner won't know anyone, maybe there he might see me in my Reebok Classics.*

The Fuji Rock Festival takes place every year in Naeba, a ski resort 120 miles from Tokyo, on the last weekend of July. If you're doing the international festival circuit, it's the next big one after Glastonbury. I knew the guy who ran the festival through his brother Gaz, whose blues night in Soho I'd been going to for years.

And so I got myself a job, driving a golf buggy around the festival, ferrying performers between tents, VIP areas and the stage. I didn't want the job just because Mike Skinner was playing at the festival (I knew it would be a blast whatever happened), but that was definitely a bonus; plus, there was no guarantee that I'd get to drive Mike Skinner in my buggy, anyway. I had to be more Machiavellian than that, and so I found out what flight he and his band were on to Japan, and I booked myself on the same one. This meant we were also on the same long, shuttle bus journey from Tokyo up into the mountains of Naeba.

You can see my plan. It worked, too. Almost too well. All my wishes came true and I ended up in bed with Mike Skinner from The Streets at the Fuji Rock Festival. We didn't actually have sex. But we had a great time and I fell in love with him.

That's what I thought, at least, and if you believe you're in love, even when it's based on fantasy, it feels vital and urgent to be with that person. But once we got back to England, Mike Skinner didn't want to be with me at all.

I was, like, 'What's going on?'

And he was, like, 'Stop calling me because otherwise my girlfriend is going to find out.'

It was horrible.

Three years later, in 2007, we met again when we were both playing at the Big Day Out festival in Australia. I was due on stage after him.

As far as he was concerned I was just some girl he'd boned at a festival in Japan. But I wasn't 'some' girl any longer. I was bigger and better than him, and I could tell him to get off the stage because *it was my turn now*.

I could have taken the high road, behaved well and been polite. But I couldn't manage it. I got hammered on stage drinking Jägermeister, and, after the show when Mike Skinner's manager was rude to me, instead of rising above it, I lost it. I kicked in doors, threw stuff, screamed, cried and had to be dragged away by the guys from Kasabian, who were playing on the same festival. I guess something was going on that got played out.

And, truthfully, I've never been better than Mike Skinner. I was bigger than him at that moment, back in 2007, and I was doing better than him commercially and financially, but artistically and as a songwriter? Him. He's better.

About eighteen months after the fight in Australia, I ended up hiring Skinner's band. The guys who had been The Streets played on my second album and toured with me. So when I returned to the Fuji Rock Festival in July 2009, I was no longer the girl trying to get in with the band; I *was* the girl and they were *my* band.

By then, things had become debauched. Festival season by 2009 was, for me, a haze of drugs and alcohol. I was on the road, drinking my way from gig to gig.

So, when I – along with my band and crew – was on the way to Japan, the drinking began in Virgin's Upper Class lounge at Heathrow. That's where we were when Liam Gallagher and his side of the Oasis crew showed up. (Oasis was still together in 2009, but Liam and Noel travelled separately to venues, however far away, and each had their own crew.)

We all got hammered together in the bar. We got more hammered on the plane. At some point Liam and I found ourselves together in the toilet doing something that we shouldn't have been doing, and it wasn't drugs. Then we were in a lie-down bed together.

When we landed in Tokyo, Liam said, in his distinctive nasal twang, 'What you doing now? Why don't you come back to our hotel?' He and his crew were staying in the *Lost in Translation* hotel in Tokyo, the Park Hyatt, whereas we were in a shit hole, so I was, like, 'Yeah, OK, fine.'

It wasn't until the next day when he said something like, 'No one can hear about this because of Nic,' that I clocked that he was married. I knew Noel was married and I knew Liam *had* been married to Patsy Kensit. That was partly why I fancied him. I'd grown up an Oasis fan. I was twelve when he and Patsy Kensit were on the cover of *Vanity Fair* as the coolest couple in the world, and that's who Liam was to me even twelve years later: that same cool dude. Obviously I shagged him. I didn't think of Nicole Appleton, even though I must have vaguely known that Liam was with her. When he reminded me about her existence I was horrified, even though I wasn't the one who was married or who had cheated.

It also meant I couldn't tell anyone about what had happened. Because surely part of the point of shagging Liam Gallagher is being able to tell your friends about it. It's so depressing, isn't it? Why do we validate ourselves with our sexual conquests? Men do it all the time and we resent them for it, but actually we're just as bad.

So, I didn't tell anyone – except a couple of close friends. One of whom was good friends with Jaime Winstone, who in turn was good friends with Melanie Blatt from All Saints. One way or another, Nicole Appleton had heard about what had gone down at Fuji Rock Festival that summer.

Six months later I was in my car with my driver when the phone rang. I didn't recognise the number but I did know the voice. It was Liam. He sounded awful, like he'd been up all night. 'Lil,' he said. 'I just need you to get on the phone. I've got Nic here, right. One of your mates is, like, trying to do a wind up or something and saying that you and me had it off or whatever, and I need you to speak to Nic and say that it's all bollocks.'

Oh, Liam, yes, sure, it's all bollocks. Let's say it's all bollocks – of course I'll tell Nicole that it's all bollocks if that's what you want – and not think about it too much or even at all, and then maybe it will go away and not disrupt what really matters: the people we love and rely on, the people we trust who deserve to be able to trust us in return. It's bollocks, Liam, of course it is. Except when suddenly it isn't, because if nothing inside the bubble matters, then does anything? Sure, it was only a shag and on tour at that, but the problem is, as I discovered only too well, if you keep denying and belittling your own experiences, intimate ones at that, then everything becomes diminished. It's insidious. Your whole value system shifts. Your sense of integrity gets blurry.

I didn't just begin to devalue intimacy as I became famous, I got careless with other things, too: my health for example, my wellbeing. And money.

MONEY

I don't know how much money I've made. Honestly. No one tells you and I've never asked. Once 'Smile' came out I knew I could spend money, and that's what I did. God, that was great, no doubts there. But no one told me about keeping checks and balances. No one told me how it actually works when you sign a contract with a record company, then make a record that may succeed or may well not.

Of course, I knew how much I was paid as an advance for my first album because I received a cheque for £25,000. That was in 2005, when Parlophone signed me for a five-album deal. What this means is that I'm locked into this deal, at whatever they agreed to pay me in 2005, for years and years and years. (It's been twelve years so far, and I'm on album four.) Of course, back then, I was grateful to be signed up by anyone, and it was Parlophone who was taking a risk: they might not have got that £25,000 back, or their expenses, if 'Smile' had sunk without a trace. Plus, as you make each album, you do get to renegotiate your advance depending on the sales of each previous record, but *only*, crucially, to a certain extent. *Only* within the terms set by the record company when they offered you that deal back on day one.

Many bands and artists get locked into hugely unfavourable and constricting deals, and many (including Coldplay, Radiohead, George Michael and Prince) have paid lawyers hundreds of thousands of pounds to try and get them released from these deals. This is not because they want to deprive the record company of a fair share of the pie, but because they discover that actually the pie isn't being shared fairly at all, and they want to work under their own terms.

The point is, at the beginning of your career, the record company holds all the cards. You just want in. No one explains the rules. And certainly I, like many of my peers, didn't ask enough questions or scrutinise what I was being offered closely enough. Now, of course, some of the discrepancies are more transparent – the huge pay gap between men and women, for example – but back then it wouldn't have occurred to me to ask questions about my male peers or about my own potential worth.

Not only did I immediately accept what I was offered, when it came to money I didn't even think about it properly. I'd distanced myself from dealing with money after London Records had threatened to sue me for millions of pounds. Back then, if I tried to think about those big sums head-on, I felt panicky and short of breath. The only way I felt like I could cope with such a demand was by absenting myself and pretending it had nothing much to do with me. It wasn't a good way to embark on my financial affairs and try to get to grips with them.

I did understand that the record had to make my advance money back before I would receive any royalties, i.e. extra money from further sales, but I didn't realise that the money they'd spent on sending me to LA to finish the record, for example, plus a million and one other expenses, would also have to be recouped before I received any more money. I'm not saying that that's not fair: of course a record has to cover all its own expenses before anyone gets a bonus, but it would have been helpful if someone had explained all this to me. Instead, what my management company did was set me up with an accountant. She in turn set me up at a posh bank, and they in turn gave me a posh cheque book and bank cards. Me? I wrote a lot of cheques. I often wrote cheques when using cash would have been easier, but I liked using a cheque book because it added to my view of money as having this abstract, random quality: something I couldn't grasp, almost literally. Quite often I wrote cheques to dealers when I was buying drugs.

I'm not letting myself off the hook for not being more careful or responsible. I should have taken more care. But as soon as I got my accountant, as well as *actually* assigning – and paying – her to deal with all my accounts, which is the whole point of an accountant, I also *mentally* absolved myself of any responsibility in this area, which is not. That was my mistake. It wasn't helped by no one telling me to take more care. Not my manager, not the accountant herself, not the record company, not my family, not the bank manager.

There should be an induction course for young people entering the music business – and, indeed, why aren't basic money and accountancy skills taught in all schools? Learning how to complete your tax returns and apply for a mortgage would be more useful than algebra, surely? Because it's great if you know how to write a hit song, but that doesn't mean you have any business savvy or know how to deal with what may be a sudden (and more often than not short-lived) influx of income.

I didn't. I still don't. But I'm learning to get more on top of things and take more care. The first thing I did with my advance was give my mum half of it. I owed it to her for all the parking fines I'd run up over the last few years. I'd spent ten grand on parking fees. Ten grand, *at least*. I find it hard to fathom that figure now, but back then, when I was a teenager, I behaved as if parking restrictions (or any restrictions) didn't apply to me.

I got my first car as soon as I was seventeen. I wasn't disorganised about that. I believed that if I could just get my licence and a car then that would solve everything: I'd be able to drive away from my childhood and into the future. And so as soon as I could, I bought my magic escape vehicle: the maroon Peugeot 206 from Chelmsford Car Auctions that people used to openly laugh at. Inevitably, I crashed it driving home from the auction, but not badly enough to immobilise it or myself. It just meant that my comedy car looked even more absurd.

I parked it everywhere. I was, like, 'Who put those two yellow lines there? I don't understand.'

I was, like, 'That space is just the right size and exactly where I want to be. I'm parking there.'

I was, like, 'This is my world and my version of reality and so this is what I'm doing.'

I was living at my mum's house in Islington when I got the Peugeot, and I'd set my alarm for 7.30am each morning so that I'd be up in time to inspect the post and scoop up any parking tickets that might have arrived, before anyone else saw them. They came most days.

I hid them under my bed. The fines began to escalate, the tickets turned into court orders and the court orders turned into threats from the bailiffs. All this made me anxious. Like the time I was threatened with being sued, I felt like I was living with a monster under my bed. Whenever I thought about what I knew would be my impending financial doom, my throat would begin to close up and I'd feel like I was suffocating. It came to a head when I moved out of my mum's house.

Things, as you can imagine – given the way I handled something as simple as parking my car – were getting a bit fraught between Mum and me, so I went to live with my godfather Danny and his wife Judy on Talbot Road in West London.

I was organised enough to register the Peugeot to Danny's address, which meant I could get a local parking permit, but I still ran up parking tickets, which I hid under my bed at Danny and Judy's house.

It didn't take Danny long to discover them. He phoned my mum to suggest they meet. 'Look,' Danny said to her. 'I've got a big envelope full of Lily's court orders, parking tickets and bailiff threats, and I'm bringing them to lunch so you can deal with them.'

My mum took the envelope. Coming back from the lunch she stopped to make a work phone call. She sat on a wall, by Green Park, engrossed in her telephone conversation. Still talking, she got up and began walking again – and left the package on the wall by accident. But because Danny had recycled an old envelope, it still had his address on the front, and whoever found the package was kind enough to put it in the post. The next day, when Danny sorted through his mail, he discovered that the monstrous envelope he'd just got shot of had been delivered straight back to him. He was, like, *What is* wrong *with these people?*

After the car was impounded, my mum got good at contesting parking tickets, telling various courtrooms that her daughter was depressed and insane (she had no idea that she was describing my future self), but she still had to pay a lot of them.

I don't get parking tickets at all any more. Running up that debt was the last time I took money off my mum. I paid her back and I've been earning my own money ever since – which is just as it should be. It shouldn't even be notable – it's what adults are expected to do after all – except that so often I'm accused of being some kind of dilettante: making music while living off a trust fund, as if my profession is a pastime I've been able to indulge in and got lucky with. I resent that because it's patronising and belittling and not true.

When I was working on this book and had nearly finished my fourth album, Mark Ronson invited me on holiday to stay with him in a villa he had rented in Ibiza. We've been friends for years and have worked together over the years: he produced two songs on my last record. Mark had five of his friends staying at the villa too, all guys. They all work in the music industry and all of them have made more money than me. I don't know if they've worked harder than me or are more talented or better at their jobs. I don't think so, necessarily. I think it's straightforward: they are better than me at making money. They are more focused on it and more successful at it. I watched them on the holiday. They talked about money a lot. They were competitive about it and wound each other up over it. *Oh*, I thought, *this is how the music industry works. It's boys penising off against each other. That's how the deals get higher and higher. It's not the content itself being worth more, it's whoever has the nerve to hoist the figure up the highest and wave their flagpole the hardest.*

Mark was generous on that Ibiza holiday. He spoiled us. But I began to think more and more: *Hang on. Shouldn't I be the one inviting people to come away on holiday? And hang on even more… surely, if the industry worked the right way, and I was a cannier person, shouldn't I own the fucking holiday house?*

I've never been able to stash money away or save it well. I did make one wise investment and that was buying my first flat in Queen's Park. It's the only property I own and it's where I live now, and though it's not huge for us as a family – it's a big, two-bedroom flat – it's great. I bought it once I started making money from *Alright, Still*. I couldn't buy it outright, though. It was expensive and though I could afford the deposit, I needed a mortgage. That proved difficult, because I had bad credit from my history of unpaid parking tickets. I remember thinking: *We're fucked in this country. I'm number one in the charts and earning a lot of money, and I'm struggling to get a mortgage, so fuck knows how anyone else is getting onto the housing ladder.* This system doesn't work and there is this whole generation of people wondering how they are going to buy their own home, and that's screwed up. I felt really lucky that I could do it.

It's seen me through a lot, that Queen's Park flat, good times and bad. It was my first home of my own and a refuge from fame. The whole building is set off from the road, so even when the paparazzi were at their worst, they couldn't come right up close to the flat, because the property had its own small courtyard for the residents to park in. I could get in my car without cameras in my face. It gave me only moments of freedom and privacy but those moments were crucial. Plus, I painted my bedroom walls and ceiling a dark colour called Hague Blue, so it felt like a cavern, my own safe place. Later, however, the flat's privacy was a disadvantage: when I had a stalker, he was able to lurk around the flat undetected, eventually breaking into my house and threatening me.

The flat was my home, but it also became my coke den and a kind of prison. I moved in and out of it over the years, for positive reasons – to move in with Sam – and for negative ones – to escape feeling frightened and unprotected. But I've reclaimed it now and see it for what it is: a practical, convenient, affordable and comfortable place for me and my kids to live.

In the second half of 2009 I announced that I was retiring from the music business.

More than anything, it was a good negotiating tactic to

try and improve the terrible record deal I'd accepted back in 2006. I was also desperate for a break. It felt like a natural time for me to take a step back from music and performing and do something else for a while.

The idea of opening a shop selling clothes seemed hugely appealing. I had some money in the bank and I was beginning to re-form a relationship with my sister, Sarah, who loved clothes too. So, never one to shy away from a grand gesture, I presented her with this idea of opening a vintage clothes business together.

Neither of us had any experience in business or retail, but we went ahead anyway.

Things weren't easy between Sarah and me from the beginning. Sarah was born in 1979. She's six years older than me and Mum always said that Sarah had longed for a little sister who she could dress up, and who would look up to her and love her, and be her playmate. Instead she got me: I rejected the little-sister role outright. As we grew up, Sarah and I developed different personalities, and yet we overlapped in lots of ways, too. We both craved attention, from men especially (neither of us had had attentive dads). Sarah used her sex appeal as her currency, whereas for me, back then, it was about being accepted as one of the lads. You'd think we might have got on, given that we weren't in direct competition, but we didn't. I think Sarah was jealous of the respect I got from boys, and I in turn was jealous of her looks and her clothes-horse body. She could wear anything and make it look good. Clothes became a way of playing out our feelings – nicking them from each other, claiming them, spoiling them, losing them, not returning them. As I became successful, I acquired a lot of them.

I was also the centre of attention wherever I went. Getting attention for us as we grew up was a rare thing, and because it had been in short supply its value was huge. Suddenly, I was getting showered with it. Sarah didn't care about me being a singer – she's never had any desire to be on stage – but the endless clothes that kept coming in and what they represented: money, success, approbation – *You deserve these things, Lily, please wear this, Lily, we love you, Lily, you're great, Lily, you'll look fantastic in this, Lily* – must have been hard to take.

I resented Sarah for years. I loved her, too. She's my sister. We know each other's history, we've been each other's witnesses, and we know the weight of the baggage we both carry. Sarah is brilliant and funny and clever and I wanted to repair my relationship with her. I wrote the song 'Back to the Start' (on my second album) about her, and our relationship. In it, I asked if we could start again. I thought that going into business together would be a way of doing that; a way of doing something together and carving out some kind of sweet future: two sisters, in business together, no exploitation or abuse or mind games, but just selling lovely clothes.

Even when I had very little money, I collected clothes. As I've said before, as a teenager I spent a lot of time in Portobello Market, searching out stuff. It was never about being super-chic. What excited me instead was mixing things up: hard with soft, rough with smooth, extravagance with thrift. I wasn't out looking for old Ossie Clark dresses back then, but was happy scoring a Mickey Mouse jumper or a pair of Stussy jeans, then pairing up my vintage finds with new sportswear: Nike white sports bras, baggy black hoodies and trainers. To sex it all up and add bling, I wore layers of black eyeliner and lots of gold jewellery.

My trick was knowing what worked for me. The prom dresses I wore when I first started singing suited my figure, and covered the bits of my body I didn't like. I liked teaming them with unexpected accessories: a big gun pendant and Nike trainers, or Reebok Classics and a little Def Jam bomber. It's what I did with my music, too. You hear lilting sunny tones as a song opens, and you think you're going to hear something sweet, but what you might get is a song called 'Fuck You'.

My friends used to tear out pages from *Vogue* with photos of how they wanted to look, but I never did anything like that. To me that was chasing something unattainable. Instead, I liked unpicking looks and making them my own, rather than following any prescribed trend. I like details, too. That's how I formed my relationship with Chanel: by asking questions about the details I saw.

I was invited to the shows initially simply because I was a celebrity who wore their label. I'd started shopping at Chanel as soon as I was rich enough. I'd buy a bag or a pair of shoes, and inevitably paparazzi photographs of me wearing the label landed on Chanel's PR desk.

'Who is this girl?' Karl Lagerfeld apparently asked his team when he happened to see one of the photographs. 'Why are we sending her all this stuff?'

'We're not,' the PR women told Karl. 'She's buying it.'

After that Chanel started inviting me to their shows, and I'm sure it would have stayed like that, too – me going to a couple of shows a year for a period of time (and that would have been great), if I hadn't got to know Karl. I met him by accident when I was DJing with Seb at an after-party following the September 2008 show. I was looking for the loo and I stumbled into a room where Karl was sitting with his right-hand woman, Virginie.

'I'm sorry,' I said, as I started backing out of the room. 'Sorry, sorry, I was just looking for the loo,' I jabbered, starstruck and feeling like I'd invaded an inner sanctum.

But Karl and Virginie were relaxed and welcoming. 'No, no,' they said. 'Please, come in.' A shoe was sitting there on the table in front of them. I'd been transfixed by it in the show because it had a jade disc midway down its heel that intrigued me: I couldn't work out how the heel could support any weight with that delicate circle implanted in it.

I saw the shoe, and I said to Karl, 'Please can you explain how the shoe works, because I don't understand the physics of it. Why doesn't the jade circle snap when the shoe is worn?'

'Sit down,' Karl said, and started to draw the shoe and the engineering behind it. It was the first time I'd talked to him properly. We chatted for a bit and he told me how much he liked my music.

It was relatively soon after that that I received a phone call asking me to be the face of Chanel for an advertising campaign. Receiving that phone call was a good moment for sure. It felt amazing. It felt like I'd won. And learning about Chanel and the clothes in more detail, and how they are made, only increased my respect for the craftsmanship that goes into couture in particular, but actually any piece of clothing that has been designed and made with care and thoughtfulness. To me, that's part of the lure of vintage. It's you putting together a look, and to do it well requires some imagination or effort. I was excited to pour all this enthusiasm into the shop.

Lucy in Disguise was a sweet idea. But good intentions didn't make Sarah and I natural business partners. Our shop didn't make financial sense from the start. We should have begun more slowly with fewer overheads, perhaps launching online and building up the business before paying rent on a big space in central London. But we let everything run away from us, got too big too quickly, and we didn't run a tight enough ship. We got too much press (which created a lot of pressure), and had a documentary crew following us around the whole time, too, which I hated, and which meant we had no space to try and feel our way forward. But the bottom line was that neither of us was good at running a business.

I realised pretty quickly that we should cut our losses, and close the business.

I lost a lot of money with Lucy. I think it tallies out at about £1.5m. I've been bad at dealing with money my whole life, and because I've always felt suffocated by the thought of dealing with it, I've let other people take charge of it (as a co-dependent, this came pretty easily to me).

I know that this isn't a particularly healthy or helpful attitude, but it has at least always been counteracted by what I am good at and what I do relish, which is working my arse off to earn it. Whatever else I've done, right or wrong, in my adult life, I've always been a provider, at first for myself and then, later on in life, for my family.

LOVE

I knew Sam for years before we ever got together. He was part of the Lester crowd of my late teens. When we became a couple, the press often referred to him as 'builder Sam Cooper' or 'Sam Cooper painter and decorator', but Sam is posh. He runs a building company, but he's not up there on a ladder with a paintbrush in his hand. He was one of the guys on the boat with Lester when he dumped me from the other side of the world. They were all on a big gap year-type trip: boys born into privilege doing drugs and exploring the same hippy trail their bohemian parents had once marked out. Sam's is a big sprawling, extended family and unlike his brothers – Tarka (a musician who died, tragically, in 2008) and Barney (who runs a record label called Room 609) – Sam didn't go into the music business or the arts. He's broken that mould. He isn't a labourer, but he grafts. He's built up his building company, Bonchurch, over more than fifteen years of hard work.

The first time I thought about Sam in *that* way was at a party I gave at Claridge's for my twenty-fourth birthday. It was a year after Tarka had died and though I'd seen Sam at the funeral, I hadn't talked to him properly for ages. 'How is everything?' I asked him, before taking him off to the loo, not to do drugs, but because it was the only quiet place where we could talk. I *wanted* to talk to him. I wanted to talk to him for hours and hours and hours. I wanted, I realised, to talk to him for the rest of my life.

Nothing happened between us that night, but it was then that I first thought: *Oh my God, Sam.* Sam. Before that, I'd liked Sam but never thought about him romantically. Suddenly, it felt imperative that I see him again, and soon, and so I invited him and a couple of mutual friends to Glastonbury to watch me a few weeks later. They came. Sam says he knew something was going to happen when a group of us were sitting in the back of a people carrier on the way to the helicopter port (go Glasto!) and I put my feet up to rest across his legs. That's when he realised, he later told me, that I was definitely flirting with him. He was right. I *was* definitely flirting. I liked him a lot.

I remember thinking: *This, just being with this person, is exciting. Being in the same room as this person is exciting.* I remember also thinking: *I'm going at a million miles an hour and my life is chaotic and I can't carry on like this for much longer, and this man seems like he can offer me a different way to go forward, and it's a better way.*

Still, I didn't take Sam's way forward immediately. As I've said, it wasn't long after Glastonbury that I left London for Japan to play the Fuji Rock Festival. Sam had lodged himself into my head, but not yet into my life. In my life, I was still rushing, drinking, drugging and shagging around, and in pretty plain view of Sam, too, because the adage, 'What happens on tour stays on tour' didn't appear to be water-tight. Photos appeared in the papers showing me drunk and out of it. In one of them I'm leaning in to kiss a guy I met at Fuji – a guy called Wade from the band The Virgins. Sam, waiting for me back home, saw that photo in one of the tabloids. He didn't like it. He called me up and laid things out. 'I really like you,' he said. 'I really want to be with you, but I can't cope with your behaviour. If you want to be with me, you have to stop.'

I loved that Sam was so straightforward. *Right*, I thought, *OK then, I'll stop, and I'll put myself in Sam's corner*. 'I'll change,' I said to him. 'I'll stop running around, but you have to promise to look after me.' Somewhere in my head, my thinking went: *If I can get someone else to help me cope with everything, then I won't have to use drugs and alcohol to get me through*.

Even though we'd hardly spent any real time together, as soon as Sam said that he wanted to be with me, I went to get his keys, and made calls to arrange renting out my Queen's Park flat. 'I'm here now,' I told him, presenting my whole self to him. 'You're taking care of me.'

Sam and I were together for six years. I can't write about all the good times with him, because we're not together any more. I made a conscious decision to end our relationship and I can't relive those moments. It's not that I'm choosing not to, or at least not on a conscious level, but I can't access them any more. My brain has shut them off. Of course we *had* good times. We had a proper marriage. We looked after each other. Listen to my songs, 'Life For Me', 'Close Your Eyes', 'As Long as I Got You' or 'L8 CMMR': they're love songs, all, and they were written for Sam and about our life together.

Sam and I loved each other, and we had important stuff in common, too. We both went through our parents divorcing when we were four. We've both got lots of siblings, most of them born as a result of our parents having further relationships with other people. We were both, a little bit, the black sheep of our families: the ones who had been underestimated but became unexpectedly successful. I remember Mia, Sam's mum, saying to him when we got together, 'I would never have put money on you, Sam, to be the one who ended up with a famous girlfriend and being part of a showbiz scene. Never in my wildest dreams did I think it would be *you*.' I remember thinking, *What are you talking about?*

Sam is funny. He made me laugh. We've got a similar stupid sense of humour.

He's also neurotic. He's a control freak. He's a forward planner. He likes to know what he's doing weeks in advance. He's quite traditional. He was a safe pair of hands.

I needed that.

I loved it that he didn't overreact about things. He was calm. He didn't do drama. Quite soon after we got together, I overslept at his house and missed a dance rehearsal for something important – I think it was my performance at the BRIT awards. I was always nervous about those kinds of performances and because I was late my anxiety fizzed into fury. I took it out on Sam. 'You didn't fucking set the alarm,' I yelled. 'It's your fucking fault.' He didn't react. He didn't shout back or castigate me for being ridiculous and a nightmare drama queen. He just ignored me and let it go. He didn't bring it up later, didn't hold it against me, didn't let it escalate. That was a new experience for me. It was a relief.

As soon as Sam and I got together we nested. We lived in his flat on Great Titchfield Street in Marylebone. In the evenings I cooked, and we went to the pub or sometimes to Groucho's. At weekends we watched the cricket, which we both loved. One weekend my dad and his wife, Tamzin, left my three-year-old sister Teddie with us to look after while they went away. I remember the three of us sleeping in the bed together and thinking: *I want this. I like this.* It was like a practice run-through, a foreshadowing of our own little family.

I moved into Sam's flat in October 2009. A few months later, we bought a flat together in Great Portland Street and moved there. By May 2010, I was pregnant with George.

MARRIAGE

When I became pregnant with my first child, George, I didn't know much but I knew two things for sure: I knew that I had to protect my baby, and I knew I had to get out of London.

As soon as we knew we were going to have a baby, Sam and I started looking for a place in the countryside. Living in London and being surrounded by the media had always felt oppressive, but once I was pregnant it became untenable. I knew I didn't want my child to grow up in an environment that included photographers camping outside my house or following me around as I went about my day-to-day life.

Sam and I looked at a lot of places, many of them lovely, but as soon as I saw Overtown I knew it was the house for us. It was just what you might imagine a lovely Cotswolds house to look like: a sprawling, low-lying, seventeenth-century house built from pale Cotswold stone with huge fireplaces in nearly every room, and a cottage (that became my studio) and a couple of barns beside the main house. The best thing about it for us, though, was its location. The house was set well away from the road, down a long drive, and so it felt completely private. It looked out onto the Slad Valley, so you couldn't see a house or telegraph pole for miles. The views from it were incredible.

It was at Overtown, when I was six months into a relatively easy pregnancy, that I noticed I was spotting and bleeding a bit. Sam was in London working, but as I was due for a scan in a matter of days anyway, my obstetrician said it would be as well to push the scan forward and do it immediately. Spotting needn't be any cause for alarm, she said over the telephone, but it seemed prudent to come in early and to check everything was OK with the baby.

I drove to London the next day and met Sam at the Portland Hospital, where I was registered to have our baby and where I was having all my antenatal care. I had an external scan and everything looked fine. The baby was moving around happily. The specialist who was doing the scan asked if he could do a quick internal examination. 'Oh,' he said, looking up at me, somewhat surprised. 'Your cervix is already dilated. You may not have had any contractions but technically if you're dilated, you're in labour.'

Oh. I was twenty-eight weeks and two days into my pregnancy, so the baby was officially viable, but still, labour? Really? Babies born earlier than twenty-eight weeks can still be fine, I was told, and there was no need to panic. The hospital would do all they could to prevent the baby being born this early, as every day he was inside me would give me a stronger chance of delivering a perfectly healthy baby. There were lots of positives to the situation. And yet I remember sitting next to Sam and holding his hand and thinking: *This isn't going to end right.*

It was a secret thought, tiny and dark, and I pushed it aside. I'd just seen my baby on the monitor, kicking about, alive and well. I was being transferred to the labour ward and there were practical things that could and should be done. The first was to make a decision.

The doctor said, 'What we really want to do is prevent your waters breaking. But we have to be prepared for the fact that you could go into full-blown labour at any point. The bad news is that we're only a level-two hospital, so we don't have the appropriate facilities to look after the baby if he does come soon. We have to make a decision about whether to keep you here or move you somewhere else.'

No one seemed able to make the decision. I didn't want to be the one making the decision, and it seemed weird to me that no one was taking charge. Surely it would be sensible to transfer me to the nearest level-one hospital with all the necessary facilities? I knew that UCL was minutes away from the Portland. Couldn't I go there? I couldn't. UCL didn't have space to take me.

Then the question became: What do we do now? That was when I realised that because I was famous and also in potential trouble, I was a problem. No one wanted Lily Allen to deliver her baby too early on their watch. What I wanted was support and reassurance, but instead I felt alone and isolated. The decision was finally made to transfer me by ambulance to Homerton Hospital in Hackney.

It took an hour and a half to get there but, once I was there, action began to be taken. This was reassuring. I was put in a bed that was tilted downwards so that my head was below my navel, and my feet above. This was to help defy gravity and prevent the baby from pressing down on my cervix. Then I was taken to emergency surgery to have a stitch put in to help hold my cervix together. I was told point-blank that there was no way I was leaving the hospital until I'd had the baby. I had three months left until I reached full term. *Fine*, I thought, *I'll get settled in.*

Sam went to M&S and bought lots of nice food to stock up the fridge in my room. My dad bought me an easel and some watercolours because he was going through an art phase at the time. My mum and my sister and my brother visited me and ate jerk chicken they'd picked up from a Caribbean takeout place they'd found near the hospital. Sam set up a camp bed next to my tilted bed. It was all going to be fine.

And it was fine. For a time. The stitch held! It held for a week and a half. It held until one night Sam made me laugh and I felt it go ping.

That's when fluid started leaking out of me. My waters hadn't broken, but they were bulging, and I was now in labour proper. The theory was that prior to the spotting I'd had a really bad toothache which led to an infection, which then got into my bloodstream, which in turn infected my waters, thus causing them to rupture. Then there was another theory that I might have strep B, so I was pumped full of antibiotics, because if you deliver a baby when you've got strep B it can be dangerous for the child.

But even with the strep B worry, it was still: 'You're going to have a baby, albeit prematurely, and it's all going to be fine!' Sam was given a tour of the neonatal unit where the baby would be taken as soon as he was born, and we were told to prepare ourselves for him to be immediately whisked away and incubated. We understood. We were having our baby! I was in labour all night.

In the morning the midwife said, 'You're crowning. We can see the baby's head. Not long now.' Then some time later – I don't know how long, maybe it was five minutes, but it could have been five hours, she said – 'The cord is wrapped around the baby's neck. There was a pulse. Now there isn't. There is no pulse now.'

That meant the baby was dead. He wasn't out of my body yet, but they knew. They called it. He was dead. I could feel his little head between my legs. But my contractions weren't strong enough to push him all the way out. The doctors told me they couldn't pull him out with forceps or use a ventouse because doing that would rip him apart. He was too small, too underdeveloped for those things.

The only thing to do was pump me full of drugs to help increase my contractions. I was warned that these drugs would make me very sick and that it would still take time for them to work.

My baby was dead. I couldn't escape the enormity of that. He was physically stuck, not quite outside me, not safe inside, either. I was physically stuck, too. I hadn't been able to keep him inside me and now I couldn't deliver him. For ten hours between my baby dying and me getting him out, I entered a realm I'd never been to before. It is a realm I cannot describe or revisit, even if I wanted to. The sickness I was experiencing was consuming. I felt knocked out. I felt not human.

George was born that evening. He was cleaned up and wrapped in a blanket and a little hat, and Sam and I held him for a long time. We took photographs. We'd had our little babe and he was in our arms; it's just that he wasn't alive. Then the doctors put me to sleep. In the morning, we were discharged. The hospital needed the bed.

For me, the journey home without my baby was the saddest, most surreal few hours of my life. A mix tape that Sam had made was playing in the car at the time, and all the songs felt relevant to our situation. The Etta James song, 'I'd Rather Go Blind', was one of the songs. It became my soundtrack. It became the soundtrack to losing George.

I don't remember how we got through the days. I remember how I got through the nights. I hadn't been drinking or smoking while I was pregnant, but my self-destructive genes came roaring back into life, in spite of Sam, who was doing all he could each and every day to help me cope with (i.e. get through) the nights, because certainly I couldn't sleep.

I'd go to bed with Sam and I'd wait for him to go to sleep. Then I'd go down to the kitchen, open a bottle of red wine and drink it while smoking a packet of cigarettes. I remember feeling numb, so numb. And doing whatever that version of crying is when you don't make a sound but become sodden with constant tears. That was my routine for months.

I remember one day in particular. Sam was working. It was raining: torrential, biblical rain. I went outside, took my clothes off, got down on the grass and just lay there. I don't know how long I stayed there, nor can I explain why I did it or even if it helped. I felt like I was in total darkness. I felt like my life was black. Pure black. If I'd been in a city I'm sure I would have started going out and taking drugs to cope with the blackness, and who knows how I would have ended up. But I wasn't and I didn't. I was in Gloucestershire, in the rain, going mad.

I got ill, really ill. Five days after George died, my best friend Jess came to help look after me. I was feeling ropey, but because I couldn't differentiate between physical pain and emotional pain at that point, I didn't notice that I was running a high fever. Jess did, and she kept trying to get me to see a doctor. I refused. I told her I didn't want to see any doctors ever again. Even when my ex-stepdad Harry turned up, took one look at me and said, 'You need to go to a doctor – now,' I still refused. Somehow between them, Jess, Sam and Harry got a doctor to the house that night. He immediately sent me to hospital. I had septicaemia.

My mum knew immediately what must be causing my blood to be poisoned, 'It's obvious. There must be some of the placenta still inside her and it's infected her blood.' But no one seemed to agree with her and she had to bully the hospital into giving me a scan.

Where else do you have an ultrasound scan of your womb

but the maternity ward of a hospital? And who else is waiting there except happy couples, holding hands and waiting their turn for their standard three-month scans or five-month check-ups? And there was me, on a wheelie bed, waiting beside them. Only I wasn't pregnant. I'd been holding my dead child in my arms only days before.

My mum was right. They did the scan and the placenta was inside me. I had to have a D&C (dilation and curettage) to remove it. Even that wasn't straightforward. Because they were doing the operation so soon after I'd given birth, my womb lining was extremely fragile, and there was a risk, they told me – just before I was put under general anaesthetic – that in removing the placenta my womb lining might get so damaged that a hysterectomy would then be inevitable. *Oh, really,* I remember thinking, *a hysterectomy? Whatever.*

I didn't think, *Oh no, I don't want a hysterectomy.*

I just thought, *I don't want this life any more.*

My life has always seemed so full of extremes. Extreme highs and extreme lows. I've often been told it's extremely unlikely this or that will happen. But everything always does happen, however unlikely the odds. I probably wouldn't need a stitch in my cervix I was told. But I did. You most likely won't go into labour too early, they said, but I did. The baby will almost certainly survive, said the doctors. But he didn't.

I remember thinking when George died: *Maybe this is God's plan. Maybe I'm meant to go through all this pain. Maybe I'm meant to write about it. Maybe it will make me a better artist.* I tried to rationalise it, because if you can make even a semblance of sense of something, you hope that the pain and the mystery of it will become more manageable. Because it is a mystery, losing a baby. You're pregnant for so long and then, just as you are experiencing the miracle of new life, poof, your child is gone, utterly vanished, leaving behind only the faintest of imprints on the world, and it's all over. It feels like your life is over.

But you can't rationalise losing a child. And your life isn't over. You just keep going and, very slowly, you piece yourself somewhat back together and get on with stacking the dishwasher and loading the laundry and making the dinner and then, yes, working or writing or attending to your marriage or eventually embarking again on family life.

Your lost child is there with you always, this beautiful, negative space inside you forever.

★ ★ ★

George died in October. Soon after, Sam proposed. We'd gone to Bali straight after Christmas to try and recover a bit, and on New Year's Eve, Sam told me that he'd organised a special dinner on the beach. It wasn't quite the romantic occasion he'd imagined: the heavens opened and the wind blew and it pissed with rain. Sam disappeared for twenty minutes in the middle of dinner. Sand blew in the food, drinks fell over, food flew all over the place.

I figured a proposal was coming. It was part of Sam's way of trying to fix me. I was in a dark place after George died, and it didn't feel like that dark place would ever end. Sam knew that if he proposed to me, it would give me something to focus on. He figured I would get excited about planning my wedding, and he was right. More immediately, why else would we be sitting on the beach in the rain with him in a fluster? I was, like, *OK, can you hurry up and pop the question so we can go back to bed!* Sam had disappeared, it transpired, because he'd gone to call my dad to ask permission to marry me. He'd had a last-minute freak-out about not squaring it with Keith, now that he was seeking 'duty of care'. Keith didn't hesitate (not that duty was high on Keith's list when it came to us). Nor did I. I said yes immediately.

Like it was ever in me to say no. I was in love with Sam, but even if I hadn't wanted to marry him I would have said yes because I would have found it too awkward to say no. Saying no might have hurt Sam's feelings. It's not that I didn't want to marry Sam. I did, *desperately*. It's just that who the fuck knows what that 'want' was about: was it about forming a proper life with someone and running into the future together as a team, or was it about attaching myself to him so that someone else could now officially take up the reins of my life…?

Sam and I got married near Overtown, on 11th June 2011, at St James's Church in Cranham, Gloucestershire. I had two dresses. The one I wore for the ceremony and which was in all the public photographs, was by a French designer called Delphine Manivet. The second one, which I wore for the reception, was designed specially for me by Karl Lagerfeld and made by Chanel.

I was three months pregnant when I got married, and I felt awkward about telling Karl that news. I thought he might be pissed off by the inconvenience of my size changing and having to alter the dress. I was nervous, too, because I didn't know what sort of wedding dress Karl was making. It's not like he offers to make you a dress and then you talk through ideas and he shows you sketches. No. He just says, 'Don't worry. I'll handle it, and it'll be beautiful.'

He was right. His dress was perfect and it fitted like a glove. I loved it entirely. But it arrived just twenty-four hours before the wedding. That's cutting it fine for a bride. By then I'd formed a relationship with Delphine, who I'd commissioned to make a back-up dress so that I'd have something to wear if Karl's dress didn't fit or arrive in time. I preferred Karl's dress, but I wore Delphine's dress for the ceremony out of loyalty because we'd been together so much while she fitted and made it. It's typical of me, even on my wedding day, to wear a dress I loved less to appease somebody I then never saw again.

My sister Sarah's outfit was the one that got the most attention in the press, however. She was accused of upstaging the bride because what she wore was so revealing. Her outfit was like a signpost to her boobs. I had known what she was planning to wear. Mum, Sarah and I all stayed at a hotel the night before the wedding, and Sarah tried on three different outfits and showed them to us. She looked great in two, but seemed determined to wear the most outlandish and least flattering. My mum and I were both, like, 'Hmm, maybe that last one *where your tits are out* is a bit inappropriate.' But she ignored us and went for it anyway. I didn't care.

Sam and I had a ball at our wedding. We flew over the Cajun singer Warren Storm and his zydeco band, Lil' Band o' Gold, from Louisiana, and Sam and I did our first dance to their song 'Before I Grow Too Old'. That song was important for us. Joe Strummer had done a cover of it that I'd always loved and when I played Joe's version to Sam, he knew it immediately. Not only that, but he knew and loved the original version because he had a friend who played in Lil' Band o' Gold. As soon as he played it for me, I loved it too, and so even though it was an extravagance – flying a legendary singer and band over from Louisiana to perform at a wedding – we didn't really hesitate. They were worth it. They were fantastic and played for nine hours straight. It was that kind of party. It didn't stop. After Lil' Band o' Gold, Seb and Theo both DJed. The music went on and on. Everyone said it was the best party they'd ever been to, and I loved it too, at least the bit of it I managed to stay up for. Because I was pregnant, I wasn't drinking or smoking, and by 11 o'clock I was exhausted. Sam took me to bed and tucked me in, but then fell asleep in his clothes next to me. We woke at seven the next morning, and when we looked out of the window we could see the party still going on, and all our friends in their party clothes around the campfire. 'Let's just stay in bed,' we said to each other. 'Let's stay together in bed and let the party carry on without us.'

After the wedding and the party, Sam and I got on the Eurostar to go to Paris for our honeymoon. We didn't want to be fancy-schmancy. We wanted to hold hands and go to museums and cafés and wander about doing nothing much, but we couldn't do any of that. We were chased by photographers everywhere we went, so after a couple of days we got the train home, back to Gloucestershire, where the first thing I did was change my name.

I didn't want to be Lily Allen any more. I was done with her and what she'd become. She had tired me right out. I was Mrs Cooper now.

MOTHERHOOD

When I was a teenager and was trying to figure out what I was going to do with my life, I remember thinking back, in my fug of hopelessness, to a specific moment in 1991. I was on set in Wales with my dad when he was working on a film called *Rebecca's Daughter*. He and I were staying in a hotel and at 6.30am we were woken up, as Dad was every morning, by a production assistant coming in, running a bath and handing my dad a cup of coffee with a cheery greeting. I watched this ritual and I thought: *When I grow up, I need a job that comes with someone like this.*

It was an outlandish ambition, given that I found it hard to do anything much back then, never mind hold down any job for long but, even so, whenever I tried to contemplate my future as a young teen, that's what would enter my head: the realisation that I needed to be nannied, professionally and personally. And so it came to pass: I've had an assistant since I was twenty-one. You find what you need.

That's one reason I loved (as well as hated) fame at the beginning of my career. Managers and assistants come as part and parcel with it, and I loved handing over control to them – as well as to lovers and friends. Fame at the beginning also gave me the sense of affirmation that I longed for. I found it on stage and when people responded to songs. Sometimes people told me that my lyrics struck a chord or that I'd identified a feeling or got something right. Hearing that meant someone was listening to me and liked what I was saying. I loved that. I think that's why I was so devastated when I felt fame 'let me down'. Instead of laughing about the shit I read about myself, or ignoring it, which I can do now, I felt betrayed. That's a dangerous cycle to get into. Rely on fame? For *anything*? What a joke.

No wonder I was so eager to cast it off when I handed myself over to Sam and became Mrs Cooper. *I'm done with you now, Fame!* I might as well have declared. *You were a crap carer and a shitty lover. You didn't nurture me one bit. You were two-faced and you bullied me and it turned out I couldn't get you to look after me at all. But I'm off to the countryside with Sam now, and I don't need to be even one bit famous because he's promised to look after me and all my needs. I'm going to be Lily Rose Cooper and I'm going to live in a house with roses over the door and dogs on the sofa and a roast in the oven, and I'm going to have plenty of healthy babies, and Sam and I are going to live happily ever after.*

At least, that's what I thought back then as I settled into married life as Mrs Cooper. That, at least, was the plan.

MOTHERHOOD

★ ★ ★

Ethel was born on 25th November 2011. She was tiny and ginger and perfect. While we were still in the delivery room with Ethel on my chest, her umbilical cord not yet cut, Sam's phone rang. It was one of those sacred moments: your baby's first breaths outside your womb, but, right in the middle of it was my press agent on the phone saying, 'You've had a girl, right? I've got the *Mail* on the other line and they want me to confirm it.' We ignored the press, but told everyone in our own world our happy news. People were thrilled. Losing a child is a deeply personal thing, but it affects everyone around you. It sets off alarm bells in the collective unconscious as well as upsetting people on more straightforward levels: babies are supposed to renew our life cycle, not arrive already dead. The birth of another child reassures people. For Sam and me, Ethel didn't lessen the hole that George left, but her birth provided a kind of riposte to what before had been an unanswerable, unassailable loss.

Sam's mum, Mia, seemed relieved in her particular own way: 'Well,' she said, when Sam told her about her new granddaughter. 'At least we know Lily can have babies now.'

I had my baby, indeed. She wasn't as healthy as she should have been, but she was alive and she was mine. She was mine and Sam's beautiful bubba.

Ethel was born with laryngomalacia. That meant her upper larynx collapsed in on itself every time she inhaled and that collapsed larynx, in turn, obstructed her airway. She could breathe, but only with immense effort. She couldn't manage to take much milk in, either. A baby who doesn't feed is hugely worrying for a mum. All I wanted to do was to sit with her in my arms and have her latch onto my boob. That didn't happen. Ethel couldn't breastfeed because of her breathing difficulties. I pumped my milk instead, hoping she would drink that from a bottle. She didn't (mostly I donated it), and even formula wasn't much of a success. What I did get down her she vomited up almost immediately. She lost weight as the weeks went by.

By February, she was ready for the first of two operations to have her aryepiglottic folds trimmed, which would help her breathe and, in turn, feed. I hated the idea of Ethel having surgery, but I was desperate for her to get the help she needed. We were both unhappy. She was hungry and tired from the effort of breathing, and I felt rejected as a mum. I was almost certainly suffering from postnatal depression, which went undiagnosed because I was determined not to admit how bad I felt; if I did ever think about it, I'd assume I felt bad because I was worried about Ethel and her health. I didn't realise that these things – childbirth, exhaustion, worry, feeling rejected by my baby, not being able to breastfeed – could actually affect my brain chemistry and thus trigger depression, something which I could have and, looking back, should have, got more help with.

After the operations Ethel's breathing was much improved, but, if anything, she was even more resistant to feeding. She was done with people messing with her mouth and nose. We were told we'd have to feed her via a tube while she slept.

I was taught how to insert the tube so it went right down

into her tummy and was then taped across her face and to her back. You had to make sure you'd got it in the right place by using a syringe inside the tube to draw out a few drops of fluid then testing a drop or two on some litmus paper to make sure that the acidity on the tube came from her stomach. Even so, often after you'd fed her, she woke up vomiting, so you'd have to wait until she was asleep again before restarting the process, silently willing the milk that was slowly dribbling down the tube to stay down, to get absorbed by her little system, and help Ethel grow. The whole process was horrible. It took two people to get the tube into her, but if you were alone and the tube came out, you'd just have to get on with things: pin her down and get it back in by yourself.

I loathed having to do this. Every so often, I'd still try her on my breast. I'd sit squishing her face into my boob and she'd look at me as if to say: *What do you think I'm going to do with that?*

When she was eight months old, I'd had enough. I was pregnant again and I think knowing there was another baby on the way made me determined to tackle the situation. I took the tube out of Ethel's mouth and gently peeled away the tape from her face and neck. 'We're going to do this, Ethel,' I told her, 'you and me.' It took three anxiety-ridden days before Ethel started feeding normally, but eventually she started drinking from the bottle. After that we didn't look back.

My beautiful Marnie was born on 8th January 2013. It was an easy birth. She was healthy and fed easily from the beginning. Our little family was now complete, and it was time for me to go back to work. We needed the money, and I wanted to write and record music again.

Gradually, over the next two years, our little family started to come apart.

I shouldn't have left the nest.

I had to leave the nest.

I wanted to leave the nest.

I wish I hadn't left the nest.

WORK,
PART THREE

If writing my second album came easily, the same cannot be said about the third.

Fuck, no. It was, like, *How do I do that again?* With my second album, *It's Not Me*, I'd felt independent. I'd felt sexy. I'd felt like I owned myself, at least at times. When it came to album three, I had kids. One of them had died. I was married. I was living in a house in the country. I was bringing up babies. I was a different person. Wasn't I? Was I? Who was I again?

I was a mum, first and foremost. But I was still in my mid-twenties, and I realised I'd hardly begun my professional life. I wanted to get back to it. I was glad to be a mother, but I realised I wanted to work, too. Looking after tiny children is relentlessly tiring and at times extremely tedious. I sometimes laughed about that later on, when I was on tour. 'Why have you come back to work,' people would ask, 'after having kids?' 'Because motherhood is boring,' I joked, a line which was then seized on by the *Daily Mail* and became a story about how 'Lily Allen was now bored of motherhood', as if it were a hobby I'd taken up and put down again.

There is nothing boring about actual motherhood. That role, I discovered, is challenging and surprising and rewarding and hard, and it comes hotwired to love and pain and worry and joy. But, yeah, the daily tasks that mothering small children requires – much of that is beyond boring. That's one reason why it's so fucking tough. It's about looking after someone else's needs and leaving yours to one side. That's a hard ask for a narcissist. No wonder my dad didn't bother with it.

I wanted to go back to work because I felt stifled creatively, but working also seemed an easier option in many ways than the grinding task of tending to two very small children.

I wrote most of my third album, *Sheezus*, in the small library room at home in Overtown. I'd sit in a chair in one corner of the room, and whoever I was working with (Greg Kurstin, mostly, and sometimes a producer called Fryars who became a friend) had their computer and equipment on the other side. We'd shut the door and write all day, sometimes into the night. Because the record company didn't have to pay for studio space, they'd sprung for a chef to cook for us every evening. The kids were looked after by a nanny. I could often hear them wanting to come in and be with me. They were little back then. Ethel was one, Marnie a baby.

I know. Get over it, right? It's the struggle of every working parent: however much you long for work or embrace going back to it, leaving your kids, especially when they are young, is hard. The great advantage of writing *Sheezus* at home meant that I could see the girls whenever I took a break. That was a huge luxury. The downside was that I could hear and sense them near me all the time. It didn't help me separate work from my role as a mother.

The thing is, I don't really see that I should have had to – at least, not so much. I wanted to work, yes, but I also had to go back to earning money. We had massive mortgage payments to meet and we employed people to help us manage our lives. Our overheads were huge. This is not a complaint – we didn't have to live like that. It was a luxury we chose, but it also had to be paid for and, as the family's biggest breadwinner, the onus was on me to support the family financially. I didn't resent doing the work, and though I found it painful to separate myself from the girls, I also understood that writing music while paying someone else to look after my children was a privilege and a choice.

The bit I didn't understand, and still find hard to comprehend, is why I, as a writer and recording artist, couldn't *celebrate* my role as a mother more. Why are so many songs about looking for love or falling in love or losing love, but not about sustaining love or familial love? Why is the role of being a parent pretty much airbrushed out in the entertainment industry? Why, if you are a young female pop artist, is it so crucial to always be sexy, desirable and implicitly available? Instead, I felt this unspoken pressure (there was always a lot of eye rolling at my record label whenever I tried to balance out my working schedule to include seeing my kids) to almost pretend that I didn't have kids at all.

These were the issues I was struggling with as I wrote my third album, and they are the issues I continue to struggle with today. I find I can now face the issue a bit more squarely. I can't solve it, but at least I can grapple with it with more confidence. But, back in 2013, the dichotomy between going back to work as a pop artist and being a mother to two very young children wasn't something I could examine with any distance or objectivity. It was right inside me. It was my waking, daily reality and I found it blinding. I look back at photographs from *Sheezus* and I think: *That person there, all dressed up, her hair all those crazy colours (surely mums don't do that?), cropped tops showing off a flat stomach (no way three babies came out of that, right?) – that person is having an identity crisis.*

I didn't come up with my look for *Sheezus*. I'm interested in the visual side of my work, of course, but I told myself that I didn't have time to sit around and create mood boards. I left that side of things to a stylist called Aimee Phillips, who became my creative consultant throughout the whole *Sheezus* period. She was in charge of how my hair and make-up looked, what I wore in the videos, and my tour costumes. In other words, I handed over my entire image to someone else. And it wasn't because I didn't have time, I now realise, but because I had lost a sense of my own identity. If you don't know who you are in yourself – I'm a mum, but not just a mum; I'm a performer, but for years I hadn't performed; I'm still young but not so young, and not in terms of the music industry; I'm married but that's not something that's particularly celebrated in an industry which values availability above stability – then it's hard to know how to present yourself to the outside world, and especially hard to decide on how you're going to encapsulate it all on an album cover. I'm more wary about that now. I learned a lot about letting other people make decisions for you with *Sheezus*, especially with the first song from it, 'Hard Out Here'.

The label didn't like it that 'Hard Out Here' used the word 'bitch' so much. One executive in America sent a long email arguing why I should lose some of the references. He'd counted the number of times I'd used the word. 'I don't think a female would like another woman calling her a bitch,' he wrote.

Umm, how about the female that wrote the song? Why do you think *she*'s using the word bitch, bitch? What's insane is that he had listened to the song, clearly forensically, but somehow the song's irony – its whole central point – had gone over his head.

That, it turned out, would be the least of it. When the song came out in November 2013, the immediate response to it was positive. '"Hard Out Here" is exactly what we wanted from a Lily Allen comeback,' wrote the *Guardian*. 'This is not just a pop song,' rallied the *Observer*. 'This is a feminist text with a really catchy drum beat. This is not JUST a pop song, this is an open letter to *Mail Online*, this is a cackling wink at modern misogyny, at women's roles in 2013…'

The *Observer* was right. I'd written the song about sexism in the music industry, because I was sick of being expected to look and behave a certain way. I was sick of having my body inspected and I was sick of sexy-face. It sickened me that, as a woman, I was *expected* to make sexy-face. No one expected my male peers to do it, just as no one wrote about how thin or fat they might be looking on any particular day. I wanted the video to reflect the song's sentiment and hard-edged anger. I wanted it to show exactly what women singers are expected to do in videos, and at the same time undermine that expectation, and I wanted to do it with humour as well as rage.

★ ★ ★

I started becoming preoccupied by how much I weighed and how thin I had looked when I became famous. There was a direct correlation between my success and my increasingly unhealthy relationship with food. It started towards the end of album one, when I started doing more shoots for fashion magazines, rather than straightforward press photographs. When you start appearing on the cover of *Elle* Mexico, say, or GQ magazine, expectations about you and your body change. You walk into a studio and you can see from the rails of clothes that the fashion editor in charge of the shoot has already spent quite a lot of time sizing up your body. You're never thin enough.

As well as that, you see photographs of yourself in the *Daily Mail* or *Heat* magazine along with other female celebrities. You're being compared to them, sometimes positively, sometimes negatively. One day, you might be chastised for having cellulite and letting yourself go; the next, you're being praised, in some awful, pointed, equally misogynistic way, for your curves and for rejecting plastic surgery. It's all awful. It shouldn't be allowed. I don't even have to write about how insidious and disgusting and ridiculous and unfair it all is – this way of treating and mistreating and judging the female body. We all know. But on it goes. I feel angry about it now, and these days I take boxing lessons to keep in shape (go figure), but for years my every waking day was shadowed by a preoccupation with my size.

What a waste of headspace. What a waste of consciousness. What an insult to every person struggling with illness or poverty or homelessness; what a diss to the sunshine and the sky and the birdsong and to any number of small pleasures or preoccupations that could have more joyfully and usefully occupied space taken up with worry about body weight. But there we are: I was a young woman and I became one of the many young women who self-harm in order to weigh less.

It started with bulimia. I began making myself sick as attention heated up with my second album. In my case, it was a direct result of having my body constantly scrutinised. I'd sit in restaurants and as soon as I had finished eating, I'd be, like, *Fuck, how soon can I get to the loo?* I'd weigh things up: *Do I have too much make-up on to make myself sick?* I carried little bottles of eye-make up remover and cotton buds in my handbag so that if my eyes streamed too much from making myself sick, I could touch up my make-up. Or I'd just make sure I ate less.

It got to the point that I didn't even try to hide it from Sam. I made it part of a pre-gig ritual that we both accepted as normal. 'Oh,' I'd say. 'I can't sing on a full stomach. I get that acid reflux thing, you know? I should have waited to eat 'til after the show.' Then I'd excuse myself to make myself vomit.

I had other strategies, too. I drank a lot of coffee and smoked a lot of cigarettes in order to suppress my appetite. I took cocaine for the same reason. If I was going out to dinner, I'd take coke earlier than everyone else to stop myself eating. Sometimes, if I had a photo shoot coming up, I'd purposefully go on a bender the night before because someone had told me that your body, dehydrated of water, shrinks after you've drunk a lot of alcohol.

I flirted with Adderall (which is really just a type of speed) as a way of getting or staying thin, once I had access to prescription drugs through the 'rock docs' contacts I'd built up in my address book (rock docs are those private doctors that the industry knows are happy to issue prescriptions for sleeping pills and painkillers without asking too many questions). Or, worse, back before I was a mum, if I had three days off, say, I'd take a succession of sleeping pills to stop myself eating. I'd lock myself in my flat, take an industrial-strength pill to knock myself out, wake up twelve hours later and neck another, and so on, until three days had passed and I could emerge three-quarters of a stone lighter.

When I shot the video for 'Hard Out Here', I was still carrying a lot of baby weight after having Marnie eight months earlier. I'd become huge while I was pregnant. When Sam and I started our family, I'd stopped drinking and drugging and making myself sick. I wasn't supposed to take any strenuous exercise because of my pregnancy history, and I was still suffering from depression from losing George and then postnatally, with Ethel, and so mostly I just took to my bed – and ate – obsessively.

Sam would go to work and I'd go to the newsagent, buy five packets of biscuits and then sit or lie around all day eating them while watching episodes of *ER*. I watched every episode of every series of *ER*. I watched every episode of *The West Wing*, too. I watched every episode of that show *at least* four or five times. As the weeks and months went by, I got really fucking big. After I had Marnie I weighed over fourteen stone. I'm short and I've got a small frame so I've got nowhere to hide any extra weight. I looked like an Oompa Loompa. I didn't embrace it, not for a second. I hated it.

But whatever I felt personally about that weight – and I lost a lot of it pretty quickly once I'd had Marnie, even if the last bit didn't shift until I started substituting meals with alcohol and drugs again – I still resented being made to feel like I was too heavy for my job, and that if I didn't lose the extra pounds then I was failing in some way. I resented that I was expected to be feminine and sexy and yet instantly erase any traces of what my female body had been through carrying and birthing three babies in quick succession. It was that message that I was trying to deliver in the video for 'Hard Out Here'.

Boy, did I get that wrong. The acclaim for the song turned quickly to criticism. Twenty-four hours after the video was released, Suzanne Moore wrote a take-down piece in the *Guardian*. 'I like Allen's voice and presence and mouthiness,' she wrote. 'But I don't like racism. Even tongue-in-cheek, hand-on-slapped-black-buttocks racism. In the video [Allen] walks away from her twerking dancers. She remains in charge. They don't. Maybe I have read it wrong. But what I see is the black female body, anonymous and sexualised, grinding away to make the rent. We are not post-racism any more than we are post-feminism. This is the context into which this video falls: a white middle-class woman playing ringleader to anonymous black women. Maybe there is a knowing wink here I missed. But I haven't missed years of black women writing about how their bodies are used for white people to write their own scripts all over them.'

There it was: a woman I admired was calling me a racist. I was racist because there were more black women than white women in my video wearing fewer clothes than white me? Fuck! I hadn't even noticed the racial make-up of the dancers. They were the choreographer's regular dance troupe and she, a well-known black choreographer called Suzette Brissett, had cast them because they were good and they knew the moves and routine she was after. That was the basis on which they were chosen. (In fact, if you're counting, the line-up of dancers comprises two black women, two white women and two Asian women.) I was wearing more clothes than them because I'd just had a baby. The dancers didn't want to be in saggy black leggings, and that wasn't the point anyway. The point was that women recording artists are all too often supposed to have the bodies of professional dancers – which was the kind of body I did not have – and dress like them too. I felt that if I wore the same hot pants as the dancers, the story would have been about my love handles rather than about the song's message.

But you can shout about your intentions behind a piece of work and justify your choices until kingdom come. What matters is how the work turns out and how it is perceived. If you try and put out music with a message that delivers more than bland banalities, you can't also claim naïvety. (Though, I do claim it. With regret.)

I was upset by the negative reactions to 'Hard Out Here'. One woman, a poet called Deanna Rodger, performed a spoken word response to the video and uploaded it online. She cried while she performed her piece because I'd upset and offended her so much. I was livid when I first saw Rodger's video, because I felt like she was using me to make a bigger point (a point I agreed with, that I was trying to make and get across in the video). But once I'd got over feeling defensive, I listened to what she had to say. What she said made me adjust and shift my thinking. It made me realise that my naïvety over the video and the reaction to it was the privilege of being a white woman. As a result, I began to read about intersectional feminism. I began to learn more and I began to look at my output in a more responsible and considered way.

That's what happened in the long term: I learned and grew from negative experiences, my fuck-ups, and the shit I had to deal with.

In the short term, as 2013 turned into 2014, I was too busy dealing with the fuck-ups that arrived one after another to think much at all.

ISOLATION

Fuck-up number one happened as my management team and I were planning the *Sheezus* tour. My booking agent in 2013, and for many years before that, was a guy called Alex Nightingale, who as well as looking after and planning all my live work – my main source of income – was a close friend of mine and Ethel's godfather. I lived in the flat below him in Queen's Park and we saw each other all the time. It reached a point where I had to tell him that I didn't think things were working between us professionally, and that I was now meeting other agents to discuss working with them.

I didn't relish having this conversation with Alex. I dreaded it, hated it, and for a long time avoided it, but it became imperative. But I was surprised when he began the process of suing me for unfair dismissal and loss of earnings.

'I want a million pounds before I walk away,' he told my lawyer. It was an absurd figure. He said that he'd been speaking to a company about an arena tour for me that was worth £10m. Ten million fucking pounds?! Get a grip! There *are* bands who do £10m arena tours, but you've got to charge people £120 a ticket and have tens of thousands of people coming to each and every gig to make that kind of deal work. I'm Lily Allen, not Coldplay or Pink Floyd. I can't fill a huge arena night after night.

Everyone wanted to do the right thing by Alex and no one wanted a lawsuit. Wearily, we began the process of trying to work things out the hard way, which mostly meant paying my lawyer huge sums of money in order to pay Alex a huge sum of money, so that he, in turn, could give most of it to his lawyer. I didn't want to go to court. It was the new year. I had my third album ready for release and was planning a long tour. Being sued by your friend and colleague is a sad and worrying way to start nine months of working on the road. My beloved godfather, Roger, was also ill with liver cancer. Compared to Roger's illness, I felt like the mess with Alex could be solved. It would just take money. I paid Alex, and I then paid my lawyer a hundred and fifty grand. I paid for it with money I'd set aside for my tax bill, and hoped that I'd make enough new cash to pay that bill once it was due. (I didn't. I paid the tax bill by going into debt.)

★ ★ ★

In April, I had to leave Sam and my girls to go to America and rehearse the show for the *Sheezus* tour. I found it hard to leave. I wanted the girls to come with me, but Sam felt that the world of sound stages and tour buses wasn't a stable environment. You do sometimes see entire families on tour: pop-star parents travelling on a family bus and insisting on a kind of makeshift stability while they are on the road. Many crew workers are family men and women, and not everyone chooses to party. But Sam had a point. Together we decided it would be better for all of us if I went on tour alone, while Sam lived between Overtown and London, running his building business. I would hit the road and earn the money (and pay for the nannies).

It's daunting gearing up for many months on the road. You've got to make sure you can hold a show, give people a good time, get on with your band, stay on the straight and narrow, not descend into loneliness, nor become wayward out of boredom or wanting to connect or from desperately missing intimacy. It seemed a tall order. I was nervous about pulling it all off. I was being sued, my godfather had just died, and I had left my home and my family but was trying to stay present for my kids by FaceTiming them in the middle of my night, when they got out of bed and started their day. Then I was having to get up and put my show together.

On top of all that, I had a week of family therapy in a clinic in Arizona to get through before my first gig. Our family was doing therapy for various reasons, but the fact was that we all needed to check in with each other. Me, Sarah, Alfie, Mum and Dad all felt that we weren't getting what we needed from each other and we'd agreed that it was time to try and support each other more. It felt like a good idea to get help doing that, and to start talking about whatever had gone wrong over the years, in a calm way, on neutral territory, with a therapist making sure we could all have our voices heard.

Family week affected me deeply, and not in a good way. A lot was said. A lot of what my mum said was directed at me. I felt betrayed, not because of what she was saying exactly, but because I felt she was directing all her hurts, guilt and pain at me and me only. Mum couldn't rail at my dad because he doesn't care: it would have been water off a duck's back. She couldn't direct it at my sister, Sarah, because they are locked into a co-dependent relationship and co-dependents don't allow anything to threaten the bonds between them. And she didn't go for Alfie, I think because she felt he was too vulnerable to take it. That left me. I became the bad person at Family Week, the one who'd made everybody else unhappy.

Bad me, who was going home to pack my bags and then, three days later, leave my home and family and go on tour for nine months.

Unlike the others, I didn't have time to talk through anything she'd said with a therapist. I didn't have time to begin to recover. Instead, I felt exposed and betrayed and isolated. Therapy? It was the least therapeutic week of my life, and it was followed days later by a letter of resignation from my manager, Todd, with whom I'd been working for seven years.

Todd and I had had our differences, sure, but I respected and valued him. I felt we had a good, close, working relationship. I had relied on him professionally to help me make decisions and to steer and protect me in a difficult, cut-throat, misogynistic industry. In return, I'd been paying him 20 per cent of my earnings for seven years, which wasn't nothing. I didn't like it that he no longer wanted to work with me, but what I couldn't believe was that he ended our relationship simply by sending me a letter, out of the blue, through my lawyer. We were used to speaking all the time, often several times a day. But now he couldn't pick up the phone? He couldn't even give me warning signals or tell me that he wasn't happy with me? I felt confused by that.

I already felt super-under confident about my new work after the furore around 'Hard Out Here' and here I was, about to hit the road with zero support. I'd now lost two key players in my team, one of whom – Alex – hated me so much he was suing me, and the other so desperate to be shot of me he couldn't even ring me up to tell me he was going. I felt isolated from my whole family, especially my mum, as due to the therapy week we were now on non-speaking terms. And I had left Sam and the girls thousands of miles away.

What was the common link? It could only be me. I imagined that the bad shit happening all around me was happening because I myself was bad (and, after all, that's what had come out at Family Week: me = bad). I surmised that Todd no longer wanting to work with me and Alex suing me was because I was washed up. I felt every single one of my insecurities rage inside me. I felt like a fucking disaster. I felt like I had entered a wilderness of chaos and loneliness.

Not long after that, in case I had assumed anyone would want to work with me under any circumstances, my band resigned, too. My band had been The Streets, the band behind Mike Skinner. I'd seen them playing at a festival, liked them and poached them. The de facto leader of the band was the drummer, a guy called Johnny. Eddie, Johnny's brother, was on keyboards. They were the core band members, and for a few years we worked well together. But I realised quickly on the *Sheezus* tour that they didn't actually give a shit about working with me.

As the tour progressed, I knew there were things in the show that needed changing. That happens: a show evolves and gets better and in theory everyone is keen to do the best job. I realised that between Alex suing me and Todd leaving me, I'd let my show get out from under me. I write lyrics and the top lines of songs and I can play a bit of guitar, but I'm not a musician and I can't curate a whole show. That shouldn't matter, because a show is a collaboration anyway, but because I was feeling so insecure about everything, I'd withdrawn from taking charge of things, and let the band get on with it.

I was in a bad way, it's true, but I still wanted my show to sound as good as possible. It was mostly arrangement stuff that I wasn't happy with. I didn't like some of the segues between songs, which I felt Johnny had made sound too charty, too Radio 1, and I hated that. I also wanted to change the set list. All this requires work and extra rehearsal. In a live show, you might have four musicians on stage, but there is still a backing track and everything is carefully set, with precise timing, to 'click' with the music coming out of computer systems: you can't just stop and start things on a whim. If you want to make changes, the whole show has to be reset so that all the timings work and everything clicks in at the right moment. It's all possible, and there is time on tour to hire a rehearsal space and make things better. It happens all the time. It just means extra work, but it *should* be work to make good live music.

The band, however, didn't want to do any extra work, not with me. I felt like their attitude was: *Look, you do your make-up, put your pretty outfits on, come out and sing the songs and we'll do the rest. OK,* they seemed to be saying, *we'll indulge you for fifteen minutes while you yak on about your ideas, but we're not actually going to put anything you say into practice.* Instead, they accused me of questioning their musical integrity. Their integrity? Too right that's what I was questioning. But I found it hard to stand up for myself because, given everything that had happened by this point, I felt like my identity, my voice and my ability to control anything had fallen away. What I should have said was, 'You're a session musician playing music that I've written and I don't feel like it's being done correctly, so we're going to change it.' But instead, I capitulated, then sulked while the atmosphere turned sour.

Johnny was especially furious. By Easter he had resigned. He sent me a long email saying he'd never been on a tour that was so miserable, that he couldn't go on any more, and that this wasn't why he went into music. His brother Eddie resigned with him, and while they served out their month's notice (not a happy time, but we had gigs to play), my musical director and I, along with the help of my friend, the producer Fryars, put together another band.

I loved my new band. They were great. They were cool.

They were nice. They were experimental and yet they listened to me. 'You don't like that?' they'd say. 'Let's try something else. These are your songs, how do you want them? Let's get them the best they can be.' In other words, they treated me like a peer and an equal partner, something that as a co-dependent who was used to feeling like I didn't have much power in any relationship, I was not used to. It felt refreshing. It felt good.

It was not, however, a type of open and healthy relationship that I could roll out to the rest of my life, alas. Fuck-up had followed fuck-up in my professional life by this point. In my personal life, though, the fuck-ups were still just beginning.

SEX,
PART TWO

I have a history with drugs and alcohol, but in terms of sex, up until my *Sheezus* tour, I was pretty straight. I didn't masturbate and barely watched porn. Sure, I'd shagged around a bit, but I didn't consider myself promiscuous. But I left our family Arizona therapy session angry, sad and confused.

So here's what I did: I started exploring sex, and not with my husband. I started sleeping with people on my tour. I persuaded myself that I wasn't cheating on Sam because they were women, so it didn't count. The dancer who first made a pass at me was very open about sex. She was into S&M and she talked about all this without any shame. She began to wake me up. I thought, *Oh, OK, let's see what this is about. Maybe this will work. Maybe the reason I haven't been coming all these years is because I'm gay and I've been sleeping with the wrong gender.* In fact, I didn't have orgasms with the dancers either, but sex with them got me thinking. We were on tour. I had more time on my hands between shows than I did at home. I thought to myself: *Maybe it's time I discovered what this vagina is about… It's done the kids. It's had lots of sex. It's got to be useful for something else.*

I bought a vibrator. I had *tried* to masturbate over the years, but I had always felt, like, *Who are you trying to kid?* It was like trying to get into sexy mode with someone I didn't find remotely sexy – myself. I have the same problem on photo shoots when photographers want me to pull sexy-face. I'm, like, *Sexy-face? Sexy fucking face?* Sexy-face to me is like Victoria Wood making one of her No-Way faces. Like, *You are having a laugh, right?* But with the right vibrator – and I bought a few – everything began to become more interesting. I was, like, *Oh, OK, I'm beginning to see how this works. Oh. Ohhhhhh.* (And since you ask, if I had to pick one vibrator above all the others, I recommend The Womaniser. It can make you come in twenty seconds or, if you keep it going up there, it will reward you with ten orgasms in a row.)

At first, I felt guilty that I wasn't exploring this new territory with Sam. Our sex life wasn't great by this point – I don't think it's unusual to stop making an effort with your partner when you've just had kids and are exhausted in every way – and neither of us had prioritised making it better. Sam was quite straight and traditional and, as we know, I had always been hung up about it. It wasn't like I planned to get home from tour and say, 'Ah, Sam, darling, I've been busy, and the thing is, we're moving forward in the bedroom.' It's not like I needed a massive dildo and two dwarves dressed in spiky boots to get me off, but I was beginning to realise that I *had* been hung up and that it was all in my head, rather than because I had some crazy anatomical problem.

I thought about the life I'd made with Sam. He was happy for me to go out and be a pop star and support the family, but when I came home, I felt he wanted me to fall straight back into being wifey and mum. What I was realising was that being wifey alone hadn't been working for me. It wasn't what I wanted for the rest of my life. I wanted my work and the way I lived my life to reflect who I was, not just as a mother and wife, but in an adult way and in a sexual way. I needed to find out who the fuck I was, and I needed to come. I needed to keep coming and to stop faking it – and not just orgasms either, but as a woman in charge of her life and her work, her career and her sexuality, and her image and her songs.

That all sounds great, doesn't it? Being in control like that? Fully formed and functioning, getting off, getting things done, feeling complete, all cylinders firing. That was what I wanted. What happened was that I behaved like a hysteric. Over the rest of that year on tour I went mad. I was desperately unhappy and became intensely destructive.

I don't know what would have happened to my marriage if I'd stayed at home in 2014.

The plan, when we'd started our family, was that I'd stay at home and bring up the kids. I'd take them to school every day, sit down with them and make sure they did their homework before constructive fun, a wholesome meal, bath time, stories and bed. I'd be the one giving them routine and structure, which is what my own childhood had lacked. Socially, life would have been dinner parties at friends' houses and going to the pub.

Maybe I would have turned into one of those wives who takes pills all day, downs a bottle of wine in the early evening, and gives someone else's husband the eye then occasionally gets shagged by him in the pub toilet. Maybe, if I'd discovered something, a hobby, say, that I could have been passionate about, I would have spent my days seeing to the kids in between gardening or cooking or writing. Sam would get home from work and we'd talk about our hours apart, eat a little cake, drink a little wine, and the years would gently pass.

Who knows? I don't know. I still don't have hobbies or passions that I can get lost in. Maybe I never will. That's OK now, because I have a sense of myself. I'm back with my girls. I'm writing music and producing work I believe in. But back then, though I still drank and used drugs as a way of escaping from myself, sex was what I turned to in order to ramp things up, using promiscuity as a way to shore myself up because it made me feel wanted.

The first time I cheated on Sam, aside from my dalliances with the dancers, I slept with a mix engineer from New York. Engineer Guy was in his forties, had just gone through a divorce, and was going through his own crisis at the time. We were both taking a lot of drugs. One night, after working together and with Seb, we all went out. Engineer Guy took us to a strip club and when he and I went to the toilet to do a line of coke, he pushed me up against the wall and kissed me. I was shocked. It suddenly felt like I'd entered a different world. It was like a door opened, in that toilet and against that wall, and I went through it without protest.

I take responsibility for what I did, but there was no question that it was Engineer Guy who led the way. He was the predatory one. We've worked together more recently on a couple of songs on my fourth album, including the song 'Family Man', which is about that time, but we've never talked about what happened between us. I sometimes wonder if I'll get the kind of letter that people sometimes feel compelled to write, where they take responsibility for the shit they put out when they were using. 'Fuck, Lily,' I want that letter to say. 'I'm sorry. You were vulnerable and you were married and I seduced you against a wall when you were high on drugs.'

The fuck against the wall turned into an unhappy affair. For a few months, we'd text each other when we were in the same time zone, then get together. It was never very satisfactory. *Obviously* I got keen on him, because that's what I do. Not only that, I convinced myself that he had feelings for me, too. He didn't. He didn't feel anything for me at all. That felt horrible, but I coped with it by moving on as quickly as possible to the next thing that could divert me from the mess of myself – and now, increasingly, the mess of my marriage. Or so it became, because once I'd crossed the border into the territory of illicit sex, I was determined to explore the terrain.

I didn't fuck *everyone* I met on tour. But I did make sure that every guy I met or talked to wanted to fuck me. I became obsessed with male attention, and I didn't say no to female flirtation, either. For my New York shows, Zoë Kravitz and her band Lolawolf supported me, so I got to know Zoë a bit. We became friends.

Later in the tour, when we were in Washington, the girls and their nanny, Jess, came out to visit me for a few days, but I had to go back to New York for a day or so for work. Zoë and I went out partying and ended up kissing. I heard that later that same night she'd got down with A$AP Rocky. *Go girl*, I thought.

When I returned to Washington, Jess greeted me with the news that the girls had threadworms, and that anyone who'd been in close contact with them should take a pill or some medicine to flush them out, because it was likely we'd all got worms, too. I wondered whether I should ring or text Zoë and ask her in turn to alert A$AP Rocky about the problem. I decided against it. If the coolest rapper in the world had caught worms, albeit indirectly, from my kids, then he could probably figure it out himself. That incident made me laugh, but mostly my exploits were the actions of someone depressed and lonely and desperately crying out for some kind of attention. I was in extremis.

It got to the point where I couldn't leave a conversation or walk away from a party unless I'd convinced myself that the men there wanted to fuck me enough to let me know. Often, if I could feel the energy change between us, that would be enough. Sometimes I'd make sure we exchanged numbers and had a brief flirtation by text. Sometimes, to make doubly sure, I'd go the whole hog and sleep with whoever it was I was conquering. Often, I had to behave provocatively to make these things happen. It became a suffocating task. And, as with any kind of drug, the more sex or sexual validation I got, the more I needed, and thus, the more provocative, extreme and inappropriate my behaviour became.

Things escalated in the late summer when I joined Miley Cyrus on her *Bangerz* tour. (Miley Cyrus, by the way, is great. She's straightforward, doesn't do bullshit and she behaves like she's been touring and performing all her life – which she has. She's a real pro.) After each show, wherever we were in the US, I'd hit a strip club. It became my thing on that tour – a way to come down, and somewhere to go so I didn't have to experience the loneliness of a random hotel room. Sometimes, I went with the dancers, and sometimes I went on my own. It doesn't matter where you are in America, you can always find a strip club and they're nearly always great. They're not like the strip clubs in the UK. The culture there is different. I think it's partly about the currency being dollar bills: the ones. It gives the club a more democratic atmosphere, as if everyone is in it together. The music in American strip clubs is good, too – it's where you often hear the best hip hop; in some parts of the USA, especially in the Southern states, music and the strip-club scene are integral to each other. Trap music, a grittier kind of hip hop, originated in the strip bars of Atlanta and Houston, for example. Between the music, the dollar bills, the energy and atmosphere in the room, the clubs have a hip hop kind of vibe which doesn't feel intimidating even if you're a woman there alone.

But going to the clubs wasn't enough for me by that point. Having people fancy me wasn't enough. Getting high and feeling thin (I was eating less and less and people were telling me how great I looked, when really all I looked was smaller), and fucking men wasn't enough. Nothing seemed to reach or satisfy me. I remember waking up one morning in those dark days thinking, *Maybe it's time for heroin, because nothing else is working*.

I didn't go there. I guess on some level, even in my desperation, I knew that I wouldn't make it back, and that taking heroin would have been a slow bid for suicide.

Instead, I hired a hooker. It felt like the least personal, coldest, and least loving way to 'use' sex that I could think of. I found my hooker by using Google, as you do. I typed in 'high-class escorts' and the city I was in, then picked up the telephone. I asked for a woman. I didn't like the idea of a male prostitute putting his cock inside me. Fuck knows where that's been. The woman the agency sent arrived quickly and she stayed the whole night. I liked her, but I also had to get up early and go to several cash machines to get enough cash to pay her. She was expensive. High-class hookers are. I didn't care. I just wanted her to help me feel something. I ended up hiring her three or four times over a couple of months, so on some level she was scratching some kind of itch, but none of it gave me any real pleasure or made me feel satiated.

I wasn't secretive about how I was using sex and taking a lot of drugs. I'd talk to my hair and make-up people about what I was doing, often in front of people I'd never met before. I was indiscreet. I wanted to be found out. I didn't care that the tabloids back in the UK were running speculative stories about me. *Fine*, I thought. *If everyone thinks I'm a slag, that's how I'll behave.* Ultimately, I wanted Sam to find out. I wanted him to know. I wanted Sam to come and get me and haul me home and look after me.

He didn't.

One of the big songs on my fourth album is called 'Family Man'. It plays with the stereotype of a man leaving home and going on the road to provide for his family, and flips it around. The family man in the song is a woman. It's the mum that gets up to no good in anonymous hotel rooms. She drinks too much. She calls up hookers. The song explores the cliché that that kind of behaviour is a male thing, but maybe it's not, the song posits, maybe it's a responsibility thing and a money thing and a pressure thing. Maybe it's not a gender thing at all, but a loneliness thing, a madness thing.

In reality, it was me in those hotel rooms going through the mini bar and knocking back a load of whisky, then having a prostitute arrive and pull out her sex toys. Behaving that way was the opposite of: 'Wooohooo, I'm free, I'm going to go and fuck loads of hookers.' It was: 'I'm sad, I'm lonely and I feel like I'm on a merry-go-round trying to bring in the bucks. I've lost any sense of who I am and I'm using sex to try and jolt me awake or plug myself into my body or maybe because I'm trying to find some kind of value in a body I've been abusing and under-nourishing for a long time now.' When I look back on what I did in those hotel rooms, I don't think of my behaviour as sordid. I think of it as desperate.

I didn't go home once the *Bangerz* tour was over and I'd

finished my show commitments. You'd think that all I'd want was to see my family and get back to Overtown, but by then I was terrified of going back home and terrified of facing up to everything I'd done while I was away. I missed my kids painfully, but I felt like I'd been away from them too long. I didn't know them any more and I couldn't bear the idea of walking into a room and watching them choose to sit with their nanny instead of me. Instead, I cancelled my flight back to the UK and stayed in LA over the autumn. I told Sam that I needed to start writing album number four, and that LA was the right place for me to do that.

That, I think, was the point of no return in my marriage. Sam must have known it, too. He must have thought: *Lily doesn't want to come back to us.*

ROCK BOTTOM

And so, instead of going home, I rented a car and a huge house in Santa Monica, which I shared with two other musicians. We did do some writing there, but we also had a lot of fun, and there was no question that I was, in effect, hiding from my family and my responsibilities as a mother. It felt easier to cope with everything – my infidelities, my substance abuse and weight loss, the desperate sense of alienation I was feeling – if I pretended I was existing in a movie.

If once I had attempted to shed myself of my Cartoon Lily persona to become Lily Rose Cooper, I was now coming full circle. In LA, everything was cartoonish. I had my hair dyed in ever more outlandish colours, almost daily. My clothes were bright and even the house we were staying in was decorated in pop-bright colours, with black and white checked vinyl flooring and bright pink and green tiles.

This all reached its apogee when I went to Kate Hudson's Halloween party. I dressed up as Dr. Luke.

Dr. Luke is an American record producer and songwriter who used to run a label called Kemosabe, which was part of Sony. He's produced monster hits for Katy Perry, Rihanna, Britney Spears, Nicki Minaj and loads of other artists. In October 2014, right before that Halloween party, one of the artists he managed, a singer called Kesha, filed a lawsuit against him alleging that throughout their working relationship, he bullied and abused her emotionally and sexually. It was a horrible story. Kesha waged a long, pretty futile battle. In April 2016, the judge presiding over the case dismissed Kesha's claims of sexual assault, sexual harassment and gender violence. 'Every rape,' Justice Shirley Werner Kornreich said, justifying her decision, 'is not a gender-motivated hate crime.'

Oh, right. Got that, girls? Some rapes are *just* hate crimes, so don't exaggerate, Kesha, and say it's gender-motivated, because it's got nothing to do with you being a woman and him being a man. Get out of court, you spoilt, whiney bitch. (I hope it's irrelevant, but it's still interesting to note that the judge is married to a lawyer called Ed Kornreich, who is a partner in a legal firm that works for Sony.)

Many artists – Adele, Lady Gaga, Kelly Clarkson – most of them women, have made public their outrage over the way Kesha has been treated, myself included. Taylor Swift donated £250,000 to help Kesha cover her legal fees. I believe and support Kesha a hundred million per cent. But still, I dressed up as her abusive producer for a ritzy, celebrity Halloween party. I'd thought about it too, and gone to quite a lot of trouble to look the part. I had green scrubs made for me, complete with a doctor's badge that said 'Dr. Luke, Gynaecology Dept', just in case anyone missed my point. It was a genius costume and entirely inappropriate. I didn't care. That's how far gone I was, and how removed I'd become from any kinds of norms when it came to my behaviour. Now, anything went, especially if it caused attention and got people talking (seemingly the only currency that held any value to me then). Katy Perry was at the party, too. She was dressed as a giant orange Cheeto. I don't know Katy Perry very well, but I still find it totally, richly, absurdly ridiculous that at a celebrity Halloween party back in 2014, I was dressed as a music mogul and she looked like a Wotsit.

All the LA stars dress up and go to that party. You can't keep them away. I saw Orlando Bloom there and made a beeline for him. I've known Orlando for years through my mum and Alek Keshishian (whose sister Aleen is Orlando's agent). Alek Keshishian made Madonna's *Truth or Dare* film, and he's one of my mum's closest friends and a godfather figure for me.

Orlando was famous long before I was, and when I first got to know him I think he felt protective of me. But, not any more, he didn't. He's a flirt, Orlando. He knew I was up for it at that party. He was, too. Or maybe he wasn't. Maybe I just assumed he fancied me because it was part of my thing of having to think that everyone did. Either way, I headbutted him so hard I knocked myself out, clean cold. I didn't mean to. I was sitting on his lap straddling him, and when I tried to lean in closer to his face, my head hit his and then hit something hard behind him. The hard thing knocked me out. I was very drunk.

I came to in Kate Hudson's kitchen with Orlando and Chris Martin trying to sober me up. Chris drove me back to the Santa Monica house and in my derangement, I thought he'd taken me to a hospital. I shouted that it was grossly unfair of him, and a total overreaction.

'Lily,' Chris said calmly, 'we're in your kitchen. But are you trying to tell me something?' In the morning I found a Post-it note with his telephone number he'd left stuck up on the fridge. 'Lily,' it read. 'Chris. Call me.' I did call him. He and Gywneth had just broken up, but they were together in LA doing their conscious uncoupling thing. They asked me over for Sunday lunch.

'Hey, Lily,' Chris said, when I was there, 'come for a walk with me down to the beach.' I realised that he was doing an intervention. I guess my headbutting Orlando Bloom and passing out in front of him gave him this notion that I wasn't in a good headspace. I wasn't very chatty with Chris, but he and Gwyneth did put me in touch with their marriage counsellor. I didn't go, but it was the wake-up call I needed. I realised I was ill. I was behaving in a way that was the opposite of being sexually liberated or free. I was trapped in a cycle. I was addicted to the drink and drugs I was consuming and the sex I was chasing. I was obsessed with getting confirmation, over and over again, that I was indeed just what I felt: an object, a fuckable thing that didn't mean anything to anyone. Such confirmation, I felt, in reducing me to a shell rather than a functioning wife and mother, might help absolve me and my behaviour.

I'm not super-close to Chris Martin, but I'll always be grateful that what he did was say to me, 'No, Lily, I don't see you like that. I don't want to fuck you. I care about you. I want to be friends with you. I want to help you.'

I just wished it had been Sam. I missed Sam. I wanted Sam to help me.

I got on the next plane to London. It was time to go home.

AN ENDING

I've been to hospital a few times for my head and/or psyche. Heart? Soul? Mind? All that. Living as a pop star is a pretty sure way to experience at least some degree of mental ill-health, even if you get away with just an absurdly inflated ego. All the ingredients are there. You're given a false sense of self. You're both rewarded and exploited by people more powerful than you – often the same people. That makes you feel out of control. You're praised and bullied, often for the same thing: saying something provocative, wearing a certain outfit, putting on or losing weight, speaking your mind. That's puzzling. People talk about you all the time. Stories get leaked to the press. Privacy seems impossible. Trust becomes an issue. That makes you feel lonely and fragmented. Paranoia seeps in. It can envelop you. It's enough to drive you mad.

Your values become based on how you look, how you

sound, how you perform, what other people think, and how much or how many people want to fuck you. That makes you feel insecure, because those values are shallow and only relate to your surface being. Praise becomes cheapened too, because it's only about that same surface, even though praise is what you constantly crave and, because it isn't meaningful (and therefore fulfilling), you can't ever get enough of it. Your self-esteem can, if you're not careful and warrior-strong, become fragile and reliant on the opinion of others.

Then there are the drugs and the alcohol. In the music industry, both are in constant, ready supply. Throw in the fact that you're often far from home. You're often hungry and under-nourished, in a bid to be as thin as possible. This applies to females in particular. Most likely, you will be sexually harassed, possibly assaulted or worse, and probably by someone you are meant to trust or who purports to have your interests at heart.

Until recently, you weren't meant to talk about this kind of harassment, because you'd been made to feel that you either provoked it or deserved it and that if you did talk about it, you'd be shamed further, ridiculed and lambasted. Of course, a sea change has started since the revelations about Harvey Weinstein were first aired in 2017, but so far there hasn't been all that much noise about the music industry. My theory is that it's because artists in our industry, unlike any other, are locked into multi-album deals and are therefore locked into working relationships that can't be untangled for years. But, trust me, sexual abuse in the music industry—? What do you think? It's been happening. It's happening still.

On top of all this, as a performing artist, you're often exhausted because the job can involve a lot of travelling and a rigorous schedule, and instead of being given proper breaks you are sent to doctors (the infamous 'rock docs') who prescribe you one type of drug to help you sleep and another to wake you up. I'm generalising, of course. But still. It's a potent mix. It can drive you mad. It did me.

Most performers are young, at least when they start out. A lot are quite needy in the first place. Non-attention seekers on the whole don't tend to pursue pop stardom. If you're already somewhat on the edge before you become a pop star, if your feet aren't quite planted solidly in the ground, and your head isn't screwed nice and tightly into your shoulders, then good luck. Hold on tight.

There's no question that the *Sheezus* tour left me mentally unsound. It left me feeling like I could no longer define myself. I didn't feel like a wife. I no longer felt like a daughter or sister. I was still a mother but I felt increasingly insecure in that role. I didn't even feel like I existed in my career. When I was sober, I would think: *Who are you? What are you doing?* I didn't like being sober and thinking those things, so I'd start drinking to blot them out. All this was made worse by being on the road. I would wake up in the blistering heat on a tour bus in somewhere like Kentucky, hung over and still able to taste the cocaine in the back of my throat and my first thought would be: *I've missed five FaceTime calls with my kids. Fuck. What am I doing? Fuck! I've got to get on stage in a couple of hours. Fuck.* And, again, I would start drinking.

I wasn't drinking to riot. I was drinking to get through

the hours. I felt like I could only function if I was drinking. It's funny because in my sober life, I struggle to find and create routine, but when I'm in a period of using, it's all quite structured. It's, like, you have a little bit of food to eat in the morning. Then you start drinking, not too much all at once, but a little, regularly. A couple of hours before the show, I'd do a line of coke to lift myself up, then I'd smoke a spliff to regulate that lift. Five minutes before going on stage, I'd take a Valium to protect against a mid-show comedown. All of this was accompanied by Grey Goose vodka, which was the only thing, along with fresh lime, soda water and a packet of crisps, that I had on my rider. On tour, I didn't have much, but I had ritual and order. In my drinking and drug-taking life, I was at least quite reliable.

I first started taking coke regularly when I began to do well and was earning money. I'd look at my diary, and it would be: *What have I got this week? Oh, a festival and the BRIT awards? Let's get drugs in.* Someone would organise it and I'd hand over the cash and thus be sorted for Es and whizz. Then it became, *Oh, I don't have a big thing on? Let's get drugs anyway.* I'd go round to someone's house. People came to mine. Everyone got high.

The next level, as your fame and wealth increase, is having private doctors in different cities, and access to prescription drugs. I embraced both. I started taking Valium and Xanex and Zopiclone. Things got scary with prescription drugs, because I was mixing them up and doing them with coke, too. I would have people back to my flat, do a load of coke and then go up to my bedroom and double drop sleeping tablets. Then I'd go back downstairs and socialise until I felt woozy, then pass out. Usually, that was followed by getting up, getting on a plane and doing it all again in a different country.

Taking drugs had become normal to me, and so had taking too many drugs, often in dangerous quantities. And I was always, always drinking. I realised how bad my drinking had got one day, in one crystal-clear moment that illustrated just how normalised my intake had become. It happened in my dressing room towards the end of the *Sheezus* tour, just as I was about to go on stage. I had my vodka and soda, short on soda, on the table next to me. I was getting ready. One of the crew came in and poured himself a glass of water, took a swig, and put it down while we discussed the show. When he went back for another gulp, he couldn't remember which glass was his, with the water in it. So I tasted both. I couldn't tell, either. I tried them again. Nope, still no difference.

This was when I realised I was drinking vodka like it was water. Literally. It even tasted the same. 'Are you serious?' the guy said, forcing out a laugh. I was serious. We turned it into a dressing-room joke. What an old soak Lily is, ha ha! But it wasn't a joke. It was an eureka moment for me. I thought: *Something is wrong here, I've got to address this.* But my thought after that was: *Just not right now.* I carried on drinking.

When I finally returned home from America, in the summer of 2015, I continued to avoid Sam and family life. I'd been booked to play gigs in the UK when I returned, and in between shows I didn't always return home to Overtown. I found it hard to be there for a day or two if I knew I then had to leave again. At least, that's what I told myself. I'd stay in London instead – and get wrecked. One night I overdid it. I took too many pills. Perhaps I misjudged what I'd taken or perhaps it was just that my body had finally had enough of what I was regularly putting into it. Either way, I ended up in hospital having overdosed on prescription pills mixed with alcohol and other substances.

Clearly, I wasn't trying to kill myself because before I drifted off into my drug-induced, unconscious state, I phoned the girlfriend I'd earlier been out with. My phone call to her – I can't remember it at all – worried her enough for her to telephone Fryars, a friend of hers, too, who she knew I was close to. Fryars rang me immediately and kept me on the phone for an hour while he in turn tracked down Seb. I felt alone and isolated, but here I was asking for help and here were people getting up in the middle of the night to help me. I feel grateful for that. I feel lucky to have that. Seb has keys to my Queen's Park flat. He came over, let himself in, scooped me up and got me to St Mary's hospital. Then he called Sam.

I remember nothing about any of it.

Sam was in Ireland with the girls, staying with his dad who lives there. He flew back to come and get me. We both pretended that what had happened was an accident, the result of my being burnt out. That was true, but it wasn't the whole truth. We didn't talk about what was really going on: that I was in deep trouble, that I'd been cheating on him and that our marriage was over.

Being in Ireland at least felt safe. I like Sam's dad. I slept
for days. But then we returned to Overtown and I couldn't
stop drinking. Before I got into bed with Sam, I'd go to the
kitchen and quickly and quietly drink a quarter of a bottle
of whisky. I had to drink whisky to get into bed and go to
sleep with my husband. That's when I knew our marriage was
collapsing. There had been warning signs, of course, but we'd
ignored them.

I had returned to Overtown briefly in the middle of the
Sheezus tour for a few days in the early summer, when we were
between shows. 'Let's have a talk in the garden,' Sam had said
to me. We'd sat outside across from each other at a table.
'Everyone is really worried about you,' he said. 'Because of
your drinking and your partying.'

I was angry when he said that. I wanted to tell him
everything. As well as my husband, Sam was my best friend
and it was him that I wanted to confide in. I wanted to say,
'You know what, I have been doing all this bad stuff. I have
been drinking. I have been cheating on you. But, trust me, it
has not been a party. I'm really depressed.'

But I felt I couldn't tell him because I had to keep going.
I had to keep performing. I had to cover our enormous bills.
I had to keep stuff from him because he wasn't just my best
friend, he was also my husband. What I wanted was for him
as my husband to say, 'Enough is enough. My wife is losing
the plot. She's falling apart. She's coming home. She needs to
be with me and the kids.' Sam didn't do that. He could see
what was happening but he couldn't act upon it. Perhaps on
some level he didn't want to. Our marriage became more and

more fragile. It was breaking. By September 2015, I knew it was broken.

Who knows why a marriage falls apart? There are the reasons that you know, that you can talk about, and then there is the more mysterious part of it: the part that means you don't, or can't, try hard enough to fix things. The part that goes: *All I wanted was to be with you forever but now I can't be with you at all.*

I knew I wasn't happy being married to Sam any more. I drank and used drugs to try and help block out my unhappiness and distract me from my loneliness, even at home. I had used sex, too. I was unfaithful to Sam over many months and *of course* unfaithfulness in a marriage is a problem. But for us, it wasn't even the main problem. It was the reveal, sure, but it was just part of what was going on; one manifestation of my inner turmoil. We weren't the first couple to have to deal with infidelity, it's just we couldn't manage to get over it. Still, it's one thing to know privately that you've reached an ending; bringing that knowledge out into the open in a grown-up way is much harder. Sam and I are good at living in denial. We were both unhappy, but neither of us wanted to end things. If you're the one who does that, it's you, isn't it – you're the bad one.

★ ★ ★

I was alone at Overtown when my dad called me at the end of the summer that year. I hadn't seen or spoken to him in weeks. I told him how upset I was. I was in a state of extremis. 'I'll come over,' Dad said. 'I'll be there tomorrow afternoon. Hang in there 'til then.'

Dad didn't arrive the next day as promised, but to my surprise he walked in the day after that. He hadn't shown up when he said he would, but at least he had shown up. That meant something. 'What's up?' he said.

'I'm depressed,' I told him. I was crying. I began to speak frankly and honestly. I said things I'd been keeping buried for months. 'Things are not good between me and Sam. I've been thinking seriously about it for a long time and I've realised that we can't go on together. I'm going to suggest that we separate.' It was the first time I'd said it out loud.

'Lily,' Dad began, 'are you sure this isn't about your career?' It was not the response I was expecting. I wasn't thinking about my career. I didn't give a shit about my career right then. I was telling my dad that my marriage was over. That's what I was thinking about. I was thinking about how I was going to break apart our family unit. I hated thinking about this, but I felt that was the only way to start going forward instead of sinking deeper into darkness and despair and self-destruction. I was, like, 'Sorry, Dad? What?'

'Well,' said Keith. 'The album hasn't done great, has it?'

I paused, tried to take in what he was implying. 'Wow, Dad,' I said, 'I hadn't thought of that.'

Then I realised that he must have read an article in *Grazia* that had just come out, which stated that the reason I was 'falling apart' was because my career was over. It was a made-up article, written to accompany a photograph of me looking drunk and sad somewhere else far away from home. How about me being sad and drunk not because my career was over, but because I was *servicing* said career instead of tending to myself and my family? I'd dismissed the article. I didn't care what *Grazia* said. But now, just as I was trying to have the most meaningful and connected conversation I'd ever had with my dad, he was using it as a reference point to explain to me what I was actually trying to talk to him about, that being my abject misery. *Me*. Lily. The one hyperventilating in front of him, not the one in the article.

I thought, *Oh my God. I'm not real. I'm not here. I do not exist.* Then I thought, *Fuck.* I wanted to say, 'I can't believe I'm so lonely that the only person I've got to talk to is you, Dad, and talking to you is like *this*. Talking to you is shit.'

I'd lost Sam. I still felt alienated from my mum. I'd become isolated from my friends since going on tour. I remember thinking, *Is this it? This is it. I really am going to be on my own now.*

I tried again. I told Dad that I didn't care about my commercial success right then.

'Come on, Lily,' he said, waving his arm around, indicating the room, our house. 'This place must be costing you a fortune.'

'Dad,' I said. 'I'm trying to talk to you about leaving my husband.'

'Well,' he said. 'On that front, I think you're making the wrong decision.'

This made me furious. 'On what basis do you think *that?*' I wanted to scream. 'Given that we haven't seen or talked to each other for six months and you have no idea about what I'm going through. Given that the only real information you have is what I've just given you – that I've been struggling with my demons for a long time, but finally reached a decision to try and change my life. Your reaction is to undermine my decision? How dare you!'

He finally seemed to see how upset and distressed I was. He then gave me his best shot. 'Well,' he said. 'You'll probably find someone else before too long.'

That conversation with my dad was a low point for me. I wasn't worried about my future, but was trying to keep afloat in the present. I was thinking about my decision and the impact it would have not just on my life, but on Sam's life and on my children's lives.

Not long after that, as the summer of 2015 drew to a close, Sam and I had our break-up conversation. We went to our favourite Italian restaurant so we could talk. It was quiet, we were away from the kids, it was a neutral space. We sat in a dark corner of the room. 'You know I'm really unhappy,' I said. 'We've already stopped sleeping together, and I think we shouldn't live together, at least for a bit, at least while I collect my thoughts, because I don't really know where I am at the moment. I think we have to separate.'

We were both miserably sad. We were both in tears.

We both felt some kind of relief.

ASSAULT

By November 2015, after Sam and I had separated, I realised I had to stop my destructive behaviour and take stock. I drove to London to meet a record industry executive over dinner to talk about work. 'I'm going to get clean,' I told him. 'I'm going to go to my first NA meeting tomorrow.'

'Brilliant,' he said. 'That sounds like a great idea, let's drink to that.'

We drank tequila, too much. I don't remember how I got home or what happened once I was there, but I woke up the next morning with a bad feeling, and in a state of undress. Something didn't feel right. I rang my driver.

'How did I get home last night?'

'I drove you and Record Industry Executive to your house,' he told me. 'He took you in and about forty-five minutes later he came back out, and I dropped him at his place.'

About a week later, Record Industry Executive called me. 'I think we need to talk about what happened,' he said.

Fuck, I thought. *Fuck, I let him have sex with me and I was so drunk I don't remember.* I also thought, *Surely he shouldn't have had sex with me when I was that out of it, not right after I told him I had a drink problem and was about to start going to meetings.*

I also thought, *I don't even know for sure if I did have sex with him.* I thought, *I definitely don't want to talk about what happened, because what I really want is never to see him again, or even be in the same room with him, and I definitely don't want to work with him.* But I also felt that I couldn't easily leave, because I was aware that I was starting to look like a difficult person who was impossible to work with.

So, instead of confronting what had or hadn't happened, I said, 'Don't worry, let's forget it, it's really important that our professional relationship works out.' (It was also a lot less awkward for people-pleasing me to say this, rather than demand answers to tricky and awkward questions.)

I had to bite my lip and get on with it. I told myself, *It's OK, because I'm going to meetings now and I'm getting on with everything and I'm getting better in myself. Never mind what happened with him, because that was a drinking thing and I'm not doing that any more, so it won't happen again.*

Things *were* getting better. I downloaded the Alcoholics Anonymous app and planned my day around meetings. I went to a meeting, sometimes two, every day. I told Sam what I was doing. I told Jess. I began reconnecting with my girls. 'It's like we've got the old Lily back,' Jess said, as things began to return to normal. I began, very gradually, to reconnect with my mum, whom I had hardly spoken to since the Arizona trip. I stopped dying my hair crazy colours and went blonde. I wanted to look clean, neat, bright, shiny, new.

I started seeing a therapist, then bumped into someone I knew, not very well, who said, 'Oh, I hear you're seeing the same therapist as me,' which meant that even the person I was paying to listen to me privately was talking about listening to me privately. I changed therapists. I went to an AA meeting and shared about how bad I'd felt because I'd been so drunk that I didn't know if Record Industry Executive had slept with me or not. After the meeting someone came up to me and said, 'I know this is supposed to be a safe place, but it isn't as safe as you think. People might gossip about you because you're famous, so maybe you shouldn't tell stories like that.' That made me feel like I was choking. I felt like I couldn't speak. I felt like I was suffocating. I felt like I was getting clean, but I was surrounded by toxicity.

I wanted to get away from London, and so I went home and immediately booked flights to LA for me, Jess and the girls, then rented a house on the beach in Malibu. The girls, Jess and I spent three months there in the sunshine. It was a good decision. In LA, with my girls, I began to feel better, stronger, healthier. I began to write songs again, including 'Family Man', about the past couple of years and everything that had happened. Although the songs were about what had been such a dark period of my life, it was only when I began to emerge out of it that I felt I could begin to examine and work through it in my writing. What was important was that finally I was beginning to feel like I could use my voice again.

By Easter, I was ready to hit the studio and so I travelled to the Caribbean to meet Record Industry Executive there to work. The girls went back to England with Jess. I had been clean for six months, and I decided I deserved a beer to celebrate my sobriety. (I know. Go figure.) Going six months without alcohol had been my goal and I'd reached it, and so, at dinner with Record Industry Executive and a few other people in the business, I ordered drinks.

Once we'd finished eating, I arranged to meet up with a bass player I knew.

'What are you doing?' Record Industry Executive said, when I started to get up to go. He made it clear that he didn't want me to leave. I was surprised. It was a casual post-work dinner. Getting up and leaving was no big deal, so why was he was making a song and dance about it? It was as if he wanted to show the other people at the table that he had control over me. 'Don't go,' he kept insisting. 'Don't go. It will embarrass me if you go. Please don't embarrass me.' It was the kind of talk that became eerily familiar to hear about when Harvey Weinstein was finally held to account for his years of sexually abusing women. It's a kind of self-abasement that seems to be as important to these predators as their use of power when coercing women – a kind of dishonest and particularly creepy version of S&M.

I ignored his pleas, got up from the table and left. I met my friend in the restaurant's bar and we went to a party. I got smashed. Record Industry Executive texted me to ask for the address so he could join us there, and once he'd arrived he told me that he was taking me back to our hotel. He said he wanted to take me home and get me safe. When we got to the hotel, he put me in his room, rather than mine, explaining later that neither of us had been able to find my room key. He then left me to sleep things off and went to meet his friends at a strip club.

What happened next was this. I woke up at 5am because I could feel someone next to me pressing their naked body against my back. I was naked, too. I could feel someone trying to put their penis inside my vagina and slapping my arse as if I were a stripper in a club. I moved away as quickly as possible and jumped out of the bed, full of alarm. The naked person trying to fuck me was Record Industry Executive. He was drunk.

I found my clothes quickly. I found my room key almost immediately and ran out of his room and into my own. I didn't call Sam but I did call my friend. Mostly, as I talked to her, I blamed myself. I was ashamed that I'd broken my sobriety. I kept apologising. I kept saying, 'Of course this is what happens if you get drunk. What did I expect?'

I guess I expected Record Industry Executive to look after me. I guess I expected him not to take advantage of my weakness. I expected him not to try and fuck me when we were sober, let alone drunk. I felt betrayed. I felt shame. I felt anger. I felt confused. I hadn't had a drink for six months and when I fell off the wagon, Record Industry Executive thought it was fine to get naked with me while I slept, slap me about, and start trying to fuck me.

Even retelling the story, it seems strange. Stranger still: the next morning I didn't confront him about what had happened. I couldn't. I felt paralysed.

I saw Record Industry Executive again in LA. He summoned me to his hotel. His girlfriend was now with him, so he asked that we meet outside the hotel, like I was some dirty secret. 'I'm really sorry,' he said. 'I shouldn't have done what I did, but I'm begging you not to tell anyone. It would break my girlfriend's heart if she found out.' I listened, incredulous that he was making me feel responsible for his girlfriend's feelings. But the thing is, I *did* feel responsible – I felt responsible for what he did as if it was somehow my fault, and I felt protective towards his girlfriend. I remember apologising to Record Industry Executive right after he apologised to me. I was tearful and upset. *I'm sorry I put you in this position and that somehow I was complicit in you assaulting me,* I might as well have said. *I'm sorry I got drunk. I'm sorry I was asleep in your bed, even if it was you who put me there. It is my fault, of course it is. I'm sorry that I'm me.*

Tell you what, motherfucker: *I'm fucking sorry that you are you.*

Why did I apologise to Record Industry Executive when he'd assaulted me? Why didn't I report it? I've tried to rationalise this, but it's hard. It's murky. And though my reasons make sense, they don't make me feel good. I wish I had been braver and more courageous. Instead, I thought, *There's no point reporting it.* I was in the Caribbean when it happened, and as far as I know there's nothing the British police could do about something that happened there. Then I thought, *What would I be reporting anyway?* What was the crime? Record Industry Executive didn't rape me. Was I supposed to report someone trying it on? (Answer: yes.) Not only did I not report Record Industry Executive, but I carried on working with him. This makes me feel lousy.

But I knew I'd be labelled hysterical, and a 'difficult woman'. (No doubt I already had that label.) If I blew the whistle on Record Industry Executive I imagined he'd dispute it. It would be his word against mine, and mine was deemed unreliable. Even I couldn't rely on my own testimonies. On the other hand, he had history. He'd taken advantage of me before, hadn't he? Had he? I couldn't remember. I didn't know, not for sure. What was for sure was that he had more power than me in the music industry, and more money. He had access to better lawyers. If things went down, I told myself, he'd win.

I did do one sensible thing. When I was back in London after returning from LA, I went to see my lawyer and told him what had happened. I then signed an affidavit swearing what I'd said to be true. I thought that if the shit hit the fan in the future, for whatever reason, I didn't want anyone claiming that I'd suddenly just made up a load of stuff to avoid Record Industry Executive making some huge financial claim on me. I wanted to get what happened down in some neutral place right after it had happened. I didn't do anything with it. I just wanted it there so that no one could say in the future that I'd rewritten the past. I wanted it on record that I'd been sexually abused by someone I worked with.

Here is something else that sickens me about the whole thing: I remember saying to Record Industry Executive before working with him, 'I need a man to help me with things.' I actually said those words out loud. I'd never said those words in *any* context before, and I'm fucking co-dependent. Worse, I meant them. I felt, back then, as a woman representing myself in the music industry, that I wasn't being taken seriously – even though I'd proved myself to be a contender in said industry. I felt like the label regarded any request or query I made as the demands of a mad feminist or a needy mum. I hate it that I needed a man so much that I said those words out loud. I hate that I still think it's true that, back then, I *did* need a man to fight my corner. I hate it that the man I worked with took advantage of me when I was drunk and vulnerable and sexually abused me.

Sexual abuse is rife in the music industry. I know I keep repeating myself by saying that, but I can't iterate it enough, because mostly, even in the wake of #MeToo and #TimesUp, everyone still stays silent about it. We now know that it's all too common in all kinds of industries, but the music world, with its hierarchies and ways of doing business, offers a particular set-up that allows, and sometimes even endorses, toxic behaviour by men towards women (and of course if they're gay, then younger, less powerful men, too). As well as music, our industry trades in a potent mix of sex, youth and availability. Drugs are allowed. Money swills about. Bad behaviour is tolerated. It's rock 'n' roll. That's the point.

Young men and, particularly, young women, are seen as commodities who need marketing and managing and moulding. Mostly that is done by men. Quite a few of the men seem to take it for granted that they can sample the wares. I was at dinner not long ago with old friends who are also in the music business. We were talking about an A&R guy who used to work for EMI. One of the guys at our dinner had just seen Florence Welch and his name had come up. 'That guy?' Florence had said to my friend. 'That guy is weird. He tried to write into my publishing contract that he'd get 10 per cent of everything I earned forever. Can you imagine? And, get this, he totally made a pass at me and tried to fuck me. *As if!*' Everyone at the dinner was like, 'Him trying it on with Florence! What a joke. What a loser!'

But I went quiet. I wasn't laughing. I was sitting there thinking, *He* did *fuck me, though.*

This guy fucked me when I was twenty years old and doing the rounds looking for a record deal. It was consensual, sure. It's just that he had all the power and I had none. It's just that I was young and he wasn't. It's just that I was looking for help and he acted as if he was doing me a favour. *It was just,* I remember thinking back then, *one of those things with one of those gross industry guys. No biggie.*

But it *is* a big deal. It's all a big deal. Let's at least give it oxygen, air it out, begin to get rid of the smell of it. Let's try and teach our daughters to be stronger and more resilient, better at being less grateful, more insistent on being taken seriously, louder at saying no.

The record industry is beginning, I think and hope, to change. The silence around abuse and harassment is still resounding, but some noise has emerged. In January 2016, a singer called Amber Coffman from the New York band, Dirty Projectors, wrote a series of tweets calling out the inappropriate behaviour of a publicist who was paid to represent her. 'A very popular music publicist rubbed my ass and bit my hair at a bar a couple of years ago,' Coffman tweeted, before naming the perpetrator as Heathcliff Berru, the CEO of a company called Life or Death PR. A lot of people in the music industry read Coffman's tweet and thought, *He did what? You're publicly shaming a guy on Twitter just for biting your hair and touching your ass? For real?*

For real. Coffman had had enough. Her tweet also triggered responses from other women, who thought: *Yeah, Heathcliff Berru did that to me, too.* They shared similar experiences online, some of them recounting much more violating and frightening experiences. Coffman's record company, when she told them about what he'd done, took her seriously and stopped working with Berru's company. Berru was forced to resign. He wrote an apology online via the website, LA Weekly, blaming his behaviour mostly on his drug and other addictions. He made sure to specify that he'd never raped or drugged anyone. He checked himself into rehab.

It's not the biggest story ever, I know, but it's telling. It's important. Women are beginning to speak out. The singer Kesha didn't win her legal battle against Dr. Luke, but she refused to back down. Her female peers have publicly supported her. They believe her. I believe her. Women know what goes on, day in, day out, in their personal lives and in their places of work, and we are beginning to speak out about it.

One of the things I found upsetting about the incident with Record Industry Executive was that it made me think back to everything that I've allowed to happen. I hate the idea that there might be other things that have gone down that I've been too drunk to remember. What does that say about me? But even if there's nothing else lurking in the shadows, I think back to the times when I've said, 'No, thanks, baby, I don't want to have sex tonight,' and my sexual partners have gone ahead and fucked me anyway. And my reaction has been to quietly endure it, then let it go. And so the patterns of behaviour and response continue. Men behave badly. Women suffer, too often, in silence. I know it can go both ways, but mostly it doesn't. Mostly, it's men doing it to women. That's my experience, and that's the fact of it.

GOING MAD

When I thought about where I was in my life towards the end of 2015, this is how things looked. My marriage to Sam was over. My godfather Roger had died. I'd felt betrayed by my mum. My work had become confused. I'd left my kids, behaved badly, become reliant on drugs and alcohol, and failed my marriage. And George had died. George had died. George had died.

But I also had two delicious daughters who were healthy and well. I had a beautiful home. I wasn't ill. I wasn't poor. I had access to help. I had friends and family, even if I sometimes felt isolated from them. I felt like I'd been in trauma mode for several years, but I thought, *I'm aware of that, and self-awareness is a powerful force.* I thought, *Things are going to change and they're going to get better.* I thought, *I'm a fighter. I'm strong. The struggle is no bad thing. Good work comes out of it.*

It was time to stride out on my own with my girls, but

without Sam. I felt like I'd been through the worst, and that I could now survive anything, on my own too, without a man to push me forward. This felt like a huge step for me given my long history of co-dependency.

Those feelings all crumbled, however, when, a couple of weeks later, on 2nd October, a strange man broke into my house, intent on destroying me.

★ ★ ★

First of all, the facts.

On 2nd October 2015, at 1.30am, a man broke into my flat in London.

I was in bed with my new boyfriend, Dan, who I'd met at the Notting Hill Carnival at the end of August. I wasn't officially separated from Sam – it wasn't yet public news – but he had moved out of the flat and into his own place. Our marriage was over. Dan had stayed the night with me before, but only when the girls were already asleep – it would take another year before he slept over and the girls were aware. For once, I was taking my time with a guy. Dan and I weren't serious at that point. He'd come over after the girls and Jess had gone to sleep. We'd stayed in, I'd cooked dinner, burned it, then we'd gone to bed.

I had locked the bedroom door. I didn't want the girls stumbling into my room in the middle of the night when Dan was there. I felt guilty about Dan staying over, but despite my new feeling of independence, there were times when I still hated and feared being alone.

We were in bed talking when suddenly someone started

banging loudly on my bedroom door. My first reaction wasn't fear but panic. I assumed it was Sam. Who else could it be? It had to be a grown man because the banging was loud and urgent, and sounded angry. It also seemed like it was someone who knew the flat, because my room is at the back. We hadn't heard anyone stumbling around or trying other doors before banging on mine.

'Fuck,' I said to Dan, who was lying on my bed. 'It's Sam.' *He knows*, I thought. *He's furious that I've got a man in the house.*

I opened the door. It wasn't Sam. I experienced a split second of relief, then felt confused. I looked at the man who had been banging so forcefully on my door. *If you're not Sam*, I thought, *who are you and what are you doing in my house?* Time moved fast and slowly at the same time. I was wearing a T-shirt but nothing else, and quickly ran to the bed to cover myself.

The man was shouting loudly as he approached my bed, and though his words made grammatical sense, they didn't seem to relate to me, so really they made no sense at all. He looked distressed and angry, and there was something child-like about him.

'Where's my dad?' he shouted, over and over again. 'Where's my dad? What have you done with my dad, you fucking bitch!'

'Who is this?' Dan said.

'I don't know,' I replied.

'You know who I am,' the man shouted. 'She knows exactly who I am,' he said to Dan.

'Who is it, Lily?' Dan asked again. He assumed he must be someone I knew; an old boyfriend or someone pissed off with me from my past.

'I don't know,' I said again. I felt perplexed. I felt shocked. I couldn't connect the man with anything or anyone I knew. 'I promise you,' I said to Dan, my voice getting desperate. 'I *don't know* who this person is. But you've got to get him out of here.'

'She's lying to you,' the man said. 'She's lying to both of us.'

All this was happening quickly. I don't know how long the man was in my room for – two minutes? Three? – but I do know that it was at this point, when he started trying to manipulate Dan and convince him that I was lying, that I began to feel real terror.

That was when I thought that this was more serious than some lost boy from the street. *This man*, I thought, *has come for me. If Dan doesn't get him out something terrible is going to happen.* I could see he was holding something under his jumper. It looked like a knife.

'Please,' I said to Dan. 'I don't know him. *Please* get him out.' Dan kicked into action. Somehow, without panicking him, Dan got the man out of the room and the house. We immediately called the police. All I wanted to do was check on the girls in their bedroom, but I felt paralysed with fear. I was in shock. By then Jess had woken up, too. She'd heard the shouting. I asked her to check on the girls. I was hyperventilating. The girls, thank God, were still asleep.

That night three police officers arrived soon after I dialled 999. Their theory, given that the man wasn't a burglar – nothing appeared to have been taken – was that he'd stumbled into the wrong house in a drunken stupor, and had got in easily because I'd left the back door unlocked.

I was pretty paranoid about security back then – I still am – so it was odd that I'd done that, but I'd locked up the whole flat before making a late supper, then opened the back door when I'd burned the meal to prevent the smoke alarm going off and waking the girls. Clearly, I'd then forgotten about it. That was my mistake, but it seemed incredible to me that on the one night I'd failed to lock the door, someone had just happened to stumble past and try the handle.

But, *OK*, I said to the police and myself. *This was a random drunk guy off the street. OK.*

Once the police had finished taking their notes they left, and Dan and I went back to bed. But I couldn't sleep. The guy didn't feel random, I kept thinking. He didn't feel random *at all*.

I reached for my phone. The detective part of my brain became determined to find clues that would reveal a more plausible explanation. I looked at my Instagram page. I remembered some weird comments I'd received that I hadn't paid much attention to, but which now seemed more prescient. I found the comments I was looking for. They were written by someone under the handle, 'AlexGray16'. I googled his name and mine. What came up were a series of tweets he'd sent me dating back a long, long time. That's when I began to connect the dots. The man who'd broken in that night wasn't random. He was the man who'd been stalking me, on and off, for seven years.

I'd never, before this night, thought of myself as having a stalker. It's easy to connect everything from a long view, but when it was happening, when it was off and on and taking different forms, I didn't know that I was being harassed by one specific person, who, because of his mental illness, had become fixated with me and wanted to do me harm.

If you're famous you get harassed. You get harassed anonymously (by internet trolls mostly) and by people you're aware of or might even know a bit (tabloid journalists and editors). You have to learn to manage this kind of bullying so that it doesn't constantly disarm you and knock you for six. It becomes, and this is at best, white noise. It's *always* there. For me, it increases exponentially when I'm actively promoting my work, but even when I'm not, it's still there. Photographs get taken, comments get made, disapproval or approval is cast about any random thing: if I'm getting a haircut, say, or swimming on holiday, lighting a cigarette or climbing into a car. I'm too fat or too thin, the piece will decry. I shouldn't be smoking, the caption will read. My car is too big and environmentally damaging, an article will say. I try not to tune into it. Sometimes, I can't help but pick up on the static of it. Occasionally, I wallow in it: an activity that is destructive, narcissistic, indulgent, thankless and regrettable, but sometimes, alas, irresistible. But it also means that I'm more inured to aggressive comments on social media sites than many other people. Wearily, I've become used to being trolled.

That's why I'd mostly ignored Alex Gray's tweets or Instagram comments – but not always. Some were so horrible and aggressive that I had, over the years, noted them down and even reported them to the police. They hadn't connected the dots that I was being stalked, either.

There is no strict legal definition of a stalker or stalking, though it has been against the law since 1997, when the Protection from Harassment Act was passed. The behaviour comes in too many forms for that. But if you look up the websites that offer help and advice about it, they will tell you that a stalker is someone who becomes obsessed or fixated with someone else, someone they don't necessarily know (though they may believe otherwise), and behaves in such a way – repeatedly and persistently – to engender fear in that person. The behaviour might be 'making approaches', 'maintaining surveillance' or 'gathering information'.

A stalker might follow you, or lurk around where you live or work, watching you whenever they can. They might write to you or email you, or leave messages for you on your voicemail or online. None of these things taken singly may amount to much, but if the behaviour is repeated over and over again, it becomes frightening – paralysingly so. Of course, anyone harassing you is frightening, but a stalker's behaviour gets to you in a more insidious way because you haven't done anything to warrant the behaviour except be yourself. And you can't stop being yourself, it turns out, even if you try.

That's what I did after Alex Gray broke into my bedroom. I retreated from everything and everyone, and tried to disappear. I know I've got a history of trying to blot myself out whenever I feel unable to cope with something. I did it with drink after George died, I did it with drugs and pills and booze in the chaotic touring days after the success of my second album, and I added sex to the mix on the *Sheezus* tour.

But this was different. This time I didn't use substances: I just shut down in and of myself. I stopped seeing friends, stopped talking openly, didn't work or write. It was less a process of blotting myself out with excess but, instead, a whittling away of my very self. It was a diminishing, confusing, fracturing, damaging and futile process, and a major head fuck.

Back to the facts. The morning after Gray broke in I phoned the police to tell them my theory that it might be Gray, the person who had been harassing me over the years, who had burst into my bedroom. Three police officers came to my house that same morning. One of them was a detective called DC Angela Slade, and it was she who stayed on my case all the way through until the end. She had been part of the child abuse investigation team that oversaw the Baby P case, which made me feel weird. Was she specially assigned to my case because I was high profile and might need 'managing?' I didn't want managing. I just wanted normal, good, effective police procedure.

Gray, I felt, was a threat, but I also assumed that if he was the person we were looking for, then he would be easy to track down. If he was stalking me it was likely he'd be nearby. It wasn't a great morning. I was supposed to go to America for work, and a car was due to take me to the airport at noon. I had to say goodbye to the girls, who were being picked up by Sam to stay with him, as I didn't want them and Jess to be in the flat until the intruder had been caught.

When Sam arrived, the police listened to me telling him the story of the interloper; more crucially, they heard me leave out the fact that I had been with Dan and that it was

him who got Gray out. I think they used that information –
the fact that I clearly felt compromised and that I had hidden
something from my husband (Sam knew I was dating Dan,
but not that he had stayed over) – to later undermine me.
While they were there I also realised that my handbag was
missing. Because of my trip to the States, it had been packed
full of valuable stuff: cash, credit cards, my passport, my
itinerary – all had been taken.

I could see the police visibly relax when I realised this.
'Well,' they said. 'Now we know what happened. It was a
burglary.'

I knew it was no such thing.

After DC Slade and her colleagues left that morning, I
cancelled my trip to America.

I then called up the best close protection security person I
knew – someone I'd worked with before, and trusted. Grand
Jean got on the next train from Paris and moved in. I cleared
my diary and made sure the girls and Jess could stay with
Sam at least for the next few days. I didn't want to see anyone
and I didn't want to go outside and I didn't want my children
coming near the flat, which I felt was a danger zone. However,
there were a few jobs I couldn't cancel, and which I figured I'd
just get through somehow. One was a trip to Morocco for a
shoot for the Swedish clothing company, Vero Moda.

The photo shoot was the last thing I wanted to do,
especially so soon after the break-in, but I couldn't pull out of
it. I was the face of their campaign at the time, and was being
paid well. It had been planned months in advance.

I flew to Marrakech a couple of days after the break-in with Aimee, the stylist for the job; my assistant, Brownie; hairdresser Alex Brownsell; and a make-up artist. Aimee had come up with a concept for the shoot, which was that I was hanging out with Alex, who she'd cast as my best friend. There would be lots of hugging each other and linking arms.

I was in a bad way on the shoot. I'm usually up for it on jobs like that, and behave professionally. But I couldn't handle it that day. I found the friendship concept naff, and I was irritated at having to do lots of Christmas messages for the company's Instagram account. *Sorry? Happy Christmas? What? You want me to say what?* I could barely hear questions or instructions, never mind try and respond. I felt like I was in a fog of fear and confusion. *Put my arms around Alex like this? Why? Because we're best friends? Really? Oh, OK. My marriage has fallen apart and a strange man had just burst into my bedroom and I'm pretty sure he wanted to hurt me, but you want me to do what?*

I behaved badly. I was short with everyone. I was difficult and cross. No one could do anything right. Aimee took me aside. 'You're being really unpleasant,' she said. 'We're all doing our best. It's only six more hours, just fucking grow up.' She was right. Of course. But six hours? I wasn't sure I could make it through six minutes. I felt like I might fall apart in six seconds. I felt isolated and alone. I felt unmoored and cast adrift. I felt, like, *Oh my God, something massive and traumatic has happened, but everybody has had enough of my dramas, and who can blame them? So what if somebody broke into your bedroom and wanted to kill you? The police say it's a handbag theft, you attention-seeking, needy little drama queen. Stop overreacting and get over it.*

But I couldn't get over it. I felt like my edges were melting away.

I took myself off into a separate room to try and get myself together. I opened my laptop to check my messages. I wanted something to tether myself to, a guy rope to haul myself back to the surface of things. An email would do. What I found was a series of messages to and from Sam, still open and up on screen. *That's odd*, I thought, *I don't recognise this conversation*. Yet I could see it was about me and it was with Sam. Then I clocked it. I had opened Aimee's laptop by mistake. I was reading *her* conversation with Sam. She was updating him *about* me, my moods and my behaviour.

That's when I lost it. That's when it all started coming out. I *really* fucking lost it. I went Diana Ross. I picked up furniture and threw it. I smashed things. I shouted. I cried. I kicked walls, the door, anything. 'I'm paying you,' I screamed at Aimee. 'You work for *me*. You're *my* friend. You say you're on *my* team. But you're not.'

You'd think that would have scuppered the shoot, but somehow we kept going. More pictures were taken and indeed then used. Vero Moda ran the campaign. I look relaxed and happy in the photographs, all candy-coloured hair, not a care in the world. Aimee wrote me an email after the shoot. In it, she told me she had tried to be there for me, and that I was obviously having a very bad time. She also said that I clearly needed space, which she would give me, even though that would play into my narrative that everyone abandons me.

I didn't want space. Too right I didn't want to be abandoned. I wanted help. I wanted support. I wanted straightforwardness. *I'm being stalked right now. I want not to be spied on by my friends, too.*

I replied to Aimee with a short email. 'Fuck you,' I wrote. And that was me done, pretty much isolated all round, cut off from colleagues and friends. I may well have been attached to an abandonment narrative, but there was no getting away from the fact that my marriage *was* over, and a strange man *was* hunting me down. Nor, I might add, did I know who to trust.

Me? Paranoid? You mean you haven't noticed my nervous tic? It's fine. Just a little *twitch* I've got from all the fucking trauma and the noise; from the stimulants and the adrenalin, from the applause, the tellings-off, from all the stuff coming in that I've bought and been given – oh, lucky me – and all the stuff that I've lost, that I can't hold on to, that I can't keep close, that I can't keep safe. I felt so unsafe. I felt like I couldn't walk down the street. I felt that if I turned off the lights, someone would pounce on me. I had long felt like my psyche was full of demons. Now I felt like the shadows themselves were full of them, too.

As soon as I got back from Morocco, I started to chart my history with Alex Gray in detail, writing down exactly what he'd been doing to me over the years. I was sure that the man who'd come crashing into my room was him, and that the night I left my door unlocked was not the first night he'd been skulking around the flat. I was determined to connect every single dot in what I now began to realise was a seven-year history of incidents.

SOMEONE ELSE'S MADNESS

Alex Gray first made contact with me on Twitter. In 2008, he sent me a series of tweets saying he'd written my song 'The Fear', a demo version of which I'd put on my Myspace page in April of that year (the song wasn't officially released until January 2009). I'm used to receiving horrible, hostile messages on social media, but I noticed these tweets more than others because the writer's Twitter handle was @lilyallenisRIP.

The next incident happened later that year. My assistant, Victoria, was working in my flat when the doorbell rang. When she answered the door it was a man she didn't recognise. 'My name's Alex,' he said. 'I'm a friend of Lily's. Is she in?' Victoria told the caller I was out, but before she could shut the door, he grabbed a pile of mail from inside the hallway, then ran off.

Victoria immediately called me, and as soon as I got home

we called the police. The police didn't come to the flat to see me about this and I didn't ask them to. I didn't connect the incident with the @lilyallenisRIP tweeter. Those tweets, posted online months before, had alarmed me enough to look at the sender's profile page and see his name there, but that name didn't lodge in my head. 'Alex' didn't strike any chords back then. I didn't like the idea of someone stealing my mail, obviously, but I assumed it was a 'fan' who knew where I lived because he'd seen the paparazzi outside day and night (waiting for me, watching me, lurking around and, you might say, also harassing me as I went about my private life in my private home).

After that, letters started arriving. They were rants – about 'The Fear' and how he'd written it and I'd stolen it, and about how he was disappointed with the social system and his mistreatment by doctors, and that I'd contributed to that mistreatment. The letters were written in small handwriting in a tightly wound spiral and they were sinister. Gray didn't just post them to my home address: he dropped them off at my clothes shop, at my record company, and my manager's office, too.

I called the police again. They came to my flat and I told them about what had now become a pattern of behaviour connected to one person. They took a statement and, as requested, I gave them the letters. They told me that if anything else suspicious happened, I should call 999.

In January 2009, I was playing a concert at a small venue in Camden called KOKO. 'The Fear' had just been officially released and it was climbing the charts (a week later it would knock Lady Gaga off the top spot and remain at number one for four weeks). Things were going well.

I was on stage mid-song when I saw it: a banner held up by a man, with the words: 'I WROTE THE FEAR. WHERE'S MY MONEY?'

I knew it was the letter-writer. I was immediately frightened and I worried that he might have a weapon. I realised, too, that I was the only person at that moment who knew the significance of that banner. I didn't like it that he knew I'd know, and that we were therefore connected by this shared knowledge. Still, I didn't freeze or panic. I finished the song, then left the stage. 'He's there,' I said to Victoria. 'In the crowd. With a banner.' She knew who I was talking about. Once again, we rang the police.

The police came to my flat the next day. There wasn't much they could do, they said, because holding up a nasty banner at a concert isn't a crime. They did, in light of not just the banner but the letters and the tweets, offer to install a panic alarm at my flat and at Overtown, and I accepted that offer. To try and make myself feel safer, I took my own practical measures, too. I made sure my flat was super-secure. I had metal grilles installed on the windows at the front, bars put on the windows at the back, and sensor alarms on the doors. When I was due to play live, I hired extra security.

These things were expensive, but I was lucky because I could afford them. Most people don't have the same resources. I did all this and still didn't feel safe, so how, I still wonder, do women in the same situation feel when they have no way of protecting themselves? I also wanted to arm myself mentally and feel more prepared in my head, so I asked the police, who by this point had told me that they knew who it was who had held up the banner (he'd been involved in an entirely separate altercation and had a history of mental illness), if I could see a photograph of Alex Gray. They said no initially, but then relented and came to my flat, quickly showed me a photo of him and then left, taking the photo with them.

The photograph wasn't of someone I recognised, and nor did I find his face memorable. Even if it scared me when I looked at the picture, I couldn't keep the fleeting image of Gray in my head.

Six months after installing the alarms, the police removed them, because things had gone quiet and there had been no further incidents.

I was relieved. I assumed I'd been given the all-clear and I tried to tell myself that I had nothing more to worry about. What I now know is that the reason Gray went quiet was because he was institutionalised over this period of time. The next I knew of him was when he burst into my bedroom in October 2015.

After the disastrous trip to Marrakech, Seb and I went to DJ for a Chanel party at the Saatchi Gallery. Dan was with us too, and when we got back to the flat late that night, there was something sitting on the bonnet of my car.

'Isn't that your bag, Lily?' said Dan.

I froze. It was the bag that had been stolen from my flat

nine days before. It had been burned, and was a blackened shell. My passport and credit cards had been cut up and were inside the shell.

I called the police once again, and once again they came to my flat. I knew Gray had to be lurking around my house and I felt scared. I felt vulnerable. I felt alone. I felt small and disempowered, and I felt like this malign force had entered my life and I had no power over it whatsoever.

This is an odd feeling. It is terrifying. Of course, things happen to all of us that are beyond our control and none of us like it. Lester left me: I couldn't control that, and I hated it. I ended up in hospital after taking an overdose of pills. But even that – idiotic and self-destructive as it was – was my way of trying to manage the situation. *Come back, Lester,* I was shouting. *Help me, someone. I'm drowning here with my heart broken and what I thought was my future pulled out from under my feet.* And someone did hear me and did help. My mum put me in hospital and slowly I got better. My heart mended. My future lay wide open again, for me to walk towards on my own two feet, and that's what I did – at least for a bit. You get rejected from a job you really wanted; the person you most desire doesn't return your call; you can't resist a drink even if alcohol is off-limits; a loved one dies unexpectedly; your baby's heart stops just as it should be beating hardest. Things happen all the time that feel out of our control, but they are still to do with us. They aren't foreign to our psyche, however unwelcome. We live with risk, and death overshadows us all.

This was different. This was outside my orbit. I hadn't

triggered any part of this, at least not in any conscious or direct way. It felt like there was this scary, malevolent force coming for me, but I didn't know from which direction. I felt like this man, with his knife under his jumper and his box of matches, and his scissors and his loud, disturbed screaming, was watching me and waiting for another chance to get at me.

It affected me hugely. It violated every area of my psyche. It made me feel scared and paranoid. It made me feel mad, like I was being slowly gaslit, because I didn't feel that the police – who were still insisting what had happened was a straightforward burglary – had been helping me at all. If Gray was hanging out outside my flat, why hadn't he been caught?

The returned handbag at last triggered the police into action. The next morning they installed CCTV outside my flat, and the day after that they found Alex Gray and arrested him. I felt relief at that news.

I assumed I'd be asked to come into the police station to identify Gray and make sure that the man they'd caught was indeed the same man who had broken into my bedroom, but the police said they didn't need my help. I found that odd. I went, uninvited, to the court the next day to witness Gray's bail hearing. I wanted to know if he would be released on bail – I no longer trusted the police to let me know what was happening.

As soon as Gray was brought up from the cells, he made eye contact with me and started shouting. It was paranoid ranting, very loud.

'Why should I grant you bail?' the judge said to Gray, once he had stopped shouting.

'Because the world would be a better place without her,' Gray said, pointing at me. 'And that's what I'm here to do.'

I was glad Gray had said that in front of the judge. The police weren't in the courtroom that day, so they didn't witness this threat, but the judge did, and he didn't grant Gray bail. He could see that he was dangerous. That's when I decided to attend all Gray's court sessions and the trial. It was important for me to have as much information as possible so that I could begin to feel more in control of what was going on. I also felt that if my being there provoked Gray to shout more or rant and rave, it would help the court and the judge see how serious the situation was.

I hired a lawyer, too, something most victims of stalking can't afford to do. I did it primarily to ensure that a harassment charge was added to Gray's sheet, rather than just the burglary charge (I felt very strongly about this, because what was the point of putting Gray behind bars for stealing a handbag when what he needed was proper medical help in a psychiatric hospital?). I knew that I would have questions arising from the trial, which was due to take place six months after Gray's arrest. Hiring a lawyer was a way of empowering myself. I knew that I couldn't simply raise my voice if something was being misrepresented or if information was not being aired. A professional representative in court meant I felt like I had a hold on the situation.

Through my lawyer, I asked to see the spiralled letters Gray had sent me years before, that I had given to the police. I knew they were crucial in terms of proving how long Gray had been actively stalking me, not just online, but in person, and I wanted the prosecuting lawyers to have them as evidence. Instead of the letters, however, my lawyer received an email: 'The letters you refer to in your letter dated 14th March have been sought,' the email reads. 'They have been destroyed in line with police procedure.'

To me, the email and the act of destroying the letters confirmed how the police had never taken me or anything I'd reported seriously. I felt angry about that, angry and distressed. Why would evidence be destroyed like that? Why would no one explain why? How was this in line with police procedure? I didn't understand, and the police on the case refused to enlighten me or my lawyer.

That's one of the problems with stalking. It may be hard to define legally, but if it's happening to you, there is nothing vague about its threat. Despite this, not enough is done, and all too often it's not taken seriously by the authorities. And yet, it's happening too frequently to too many of us.

According to Paladin, the National Stalking Advocacy Service, one in five women and one in ten men will experience stalking in their adult lives. Most don't report it to the police until they've been harassed at least a hundred times. Even then, not much seems to be done: only 1 per cent of stalking and 16 per cent of harassment cases result in a charge and prosecution by the CPS – but that's only of the cases that make it to the police in the first place. Many women (80 per cent of the victims are women) don't report the crime at all. But not reporting a crime doesn't mean you aren't suffering. It's a crime with very real consequences. Stalking, as well as engendering fear in its victims – crime enough – often leads to violence, and sometimes to murder.

It turned out that I was one of the lucky ones. My stalker had been caught and, six months after his arrest, he was going to court. It had been a battle. The file I have detailing my lawyer's fight to get the harassment charge added to Gray's charge sheet is fat with documents and correspondence. I still feel anger when I think about how insistent the police were that what I'd experienced that night in early October was a burglary, and that I was being nothing but bothersome when all I was after was the truth, which was that I had a stalker. Gray had broken into my home. He was unhinged. He wanted to do me harm. I needed to be kept safe. He needed proper help. Instead, I was made to feel like I was the one going mad.

★ ★ ★

The trial was in April 2016. I attended every session. Over the course of it, I learned what was already quite clear: Alex Gray was mentally ill. In 2014, according to his mother, Michelle, he was diagnosed with paranoia and schizophrenia. She'd been battling the healthcare system trying to get her son proper help for twenty years. 'He was meant to be on medication,' she explained to the media, 'but nobody ensured that he took it. There was no follow-up. We knew he had a fixation [with Lily Allen], but not that he'd been anywhere near her. We didn't know he'd been as far as this.'

Michelle had more information for the case, too. On 9th October 2015, her son had emailed her saying: *god must want me to kill these fake cunts… they are complete scum i am here to kill some1.* The next day, he emailed her again: *i got hold of some money when i was in london guess whare from ive got a phone aswell. im trying to fucking get into it i dont give a fuck dont be surprised if i go to prison for a long time soon because im determined to murder some1 in showbiz.*

Those emails, which Michelle immediately sent to the police, were written a week after Gray burst into my bedroom, and one or two days before he was back outside my flat to dump my handbag on top of my car. The money he referred to must have been the cash he'd taken from my bag, and presumably the celebrity he was determined to murder was me. The police didn't tell me about the emails. Nor did they tell me that during one of their interviews with him, he'd said that what he really wanted to do was put a knife through my face. I found out these things after the trial when my lawyer took me into a small interview room in the courthouse and showed me the transcripts of all the evidence that had been built up around the case.

I found the information horrifying but empowering. I had wanted to know what I was up against so that I could better protect myself. I thought again and again of DC Slade's words to me as we were preparing for the trial, when I was desperately trying to get harassment added to the burglary charge against Gray: 'Whoever he is,' she'd said, patronising me, 'he's not a dangerous man.' It was bad enough that Slade was refusing to take me seriously, but given that it was after Gray had told the police that he'd wanted to knife me, it was also an outright lie.

Most victims don't have the luxury of a private lawyer to help them negotiate the court system and evidence protocols. It cost me £40,000 in lawyers' fees, which shows how impossible it is for any victim other than a rich one to afford extra legal help. Once again, it's another mind-boggling sum of money that to me felt like an abstract expense. I didn't resent paying it, but it did add to my confused sense of the worth of time and labour, and further helped devalue the currency in my little kingdom with its own crazy, escalating economy.

In early June, Gray was convicted at Harrow Crown Court after being found guilty of burglary and stalking causing alarm and distress. The judge, quite rightly, didn't send him to prison but detained him indefinitely under the Mental Health Act. He was admitted to hospital, and will remain there until it is decided that he is well enough to be released. The Home Secretary will have to sign off on this, so it's not something that can slip under the radar. Gray's illness was finally taken seriously.

STRONGER

I found having a stalker deeply disturbing. I wasn't hurt physically, but it has taken a long time for me to recover. I left my flat – the flat I'd had for seven years – days after Gray was arrested and rented a small house in a busier area of London. This meant that very quickly our family life splintered further apart. Yes, Sam and I had separated, and he had found somewhere new to live, but suddenly we didn't have the luxury of keeping the girls settled while we both took our time to find and establish proper new nests, rather than short-term places to stay.

That flat was no longer a home because it was no longer a safe place for me or my children. Any kind of family life there had now been rendered untenable. I felt like my children were in danger if they stayed in London, but I didn't want them going back to Overtown, which lies isolated at the end of a private track, without either Sam or me there. I wanted them surrounded by as many people as possible – it was as if I couldn't get enough bodies between them and the world – so I sent them, along with Jess, to stay at Soho House in Oxfordshire for ten days while I found a new London place for us to live.

It was at this time that I retreated from the world. For six months, I didn't call my friends. I rarely went out, and when I did, it was fairly disastrously. I felt exhausted and traumatised and very, very isolated. I did little work, except the work of keeping on top of the case, which felt like a full-time job. I put the rest of my energy into making a new home for myself and the girls, decorating our new rental. I fell into ill health, with most of the pain coming from my abdomen.

I was tested for Crohn's disease after I found blood in my shit, but the test came back clear and so I was sent to the gynaecologist to see if she could shed light on what was ailing me. She explained that the blood probably wasn't coming from my bowel, but was more likely to be menstrual blood, even if I wasn't expecting my period – they'd mostly stopped since I'd had a Mirena coil fitted after having Marnie. It was common, the gynaecologist explained, for women to store trauma in their abdomen and for their reproductive system to become alerted by trauma, thus triggering unexpected periods and pain. Presumably it's a way of your body shutting down and refusing to procreate when it feels in danger. Certainly, we all know how connected everything is: if you feel panicky, you feel it all over your body, you don't just think it, even if everything is going on inside your head. But what had been happening to me wasn't just in my head, anyway. My physical self had been threatened, and so I was not surprised that I reacted in every part of my body.

There is no miracle cure for feeling traumatised. I could take painkillers for my intense period pains but, mostly, to feel better, I just had to get better and heal, slowly and gradually as the months went by.

While I had worked on the case, I had waited for what I assumed would happen, which was that the story would be splashed across the tabloids. I didn't want to be on the cover of *The Sun*, not one bit, but when the tabloids stick you on their pages for buying a bicycle or smoking a cigarette or just walking out of the house and being a woman and having an arse; when you've lived with that as your daily reality for *years*, then when the fact that your home has been broken into and your life potentially threatened by a certifiable nutcase is greeted with radio silence by the press, it seems weird and unfathomable.

Every single week before Alex Gray broke in, part of my housekeeping routine was dealing with emails from tabloid news editors asking me to confirm or deny things that had or hadn't happened. *We've heard you can't pay your tax bill. True or false? Your daughter is attending this particular nursery, correct? Are you selling your house? Did you buy a car?* I got these kinds of emails every week, often every day. So the fact that no one was printing or asking me about this story – an actual true story – didn't make any sense.

I went over and over it in my head. It seemed inconceivable that the editors and reporters were in the dark. We know from the Leveson Inquiry how sticky and close the relationship is between the tabloids and the police, and how quickly information is shared between the two institutions. So what were they waiting for? Were they waiting for a conviction so that they could tailor their story? Were they hoping that somehow Gray would get off, so that I could be depicted as the guilty party? Cartoon Lily is always guilty in tabloid world. And I felt guilty, too – I was still living in a cloud of guilt and shame over the failure of my marriage.

I imagined the front cover of *The Sun*: 'Stalker finds Lily and Lover in Bed Together'. The lover, my boyfriend Dan, who protected me and managed to get Gray out of the house, is black. He grew up in Tottenham on a council estate. I didn't know much about his past back then, but I felt sure they'd find something on him to do him down. I imagined the story underneath the headline. *Poor Sam, the middle-class white guy, tirelessly bringing up the kids, has been betrayed by nasty Lily having sex with a waster from a council flat. The dirty slag. She deserves whatever she gets.* Who knows why the story wasn't in the tabloids. Was it that me being a victim didn't fit with their narrative about me? Were they lying in wait? Were they cooking up something worse?

I realised I could keep imagining increasingly horrific scenarios or I could take control of the situation. My mum and I – we had been gradually healing our relationship over the past few months – talked it over and she suggested that I email Catherine Mayer, the journalist, author and co-founder of the Women's Equality Party. Mum said that Catherine would be a wise person to talk to and would help steer me in the right direction, and she was right. It was Catherine who suggested a meeting with Paladin, the National Stalking Advocacy Agency, and she who accompanied me to a meeting to tell the women there my story of being stalked.

It was the first time I'd told the whole story, including what had happened with the police and at the trial, to anyone outside my family. Catherine and the women from Paladin were puzzled and shocked. They couldn't believe what I was saying. 'Have you got your emails to and from the police to prove what you say?' they asked. 'Have you got the letter from them saying the letters you gave them, which was evidence, had been destroyed, with no explanation as to why? Can you show us these things?' I told them that I did and that I could.

Their reaction was the first time I felt comforted. Finally, I felt like I could start to process what had happened to me. Before, I'd felt undermined at every turn, and that my refusal to accept that I'd been the victim of a handbag theft had been fuelled only by my own desire for attention and melodrama. Now, for the first time, I felt like I was allowed to acknowledge that I had been through something frightening, personal and serious.

When the meeting was over and I had driven myself home, Catherine rang me. 'Look,' she said. 'It's Stalker Awareness Week next week. We could do something that could really make a difference. Are you willing to tell the story to the press if it's handled in a responsible and truthful way?'

I said I was. What I most wanted was to get the truth on record, and this seemed the quickest and most effective way. If that, in turn, helped give oxygen to the issue of stalking at a prescient time, so much the better.

It was Catherine who arranged for me to meet Tracy McVeigh, a journalist for the *Observer*. Tracy came to my flat and interviewed me at length. She was reassuring. 'The facts speak for themselves,' she said simply. 'You've been mistreated.' Again, I felt relief. Here was another grown-up, sensible woman saying to me: *This isn't right. Your feelings are appropriate. You're clearly vulnerable and you've been gaslit.*

That Sunday, I was on the front cover of the *Observer* newspaper and its magazine. The story was the magazine's main feature. That front page of the *Observer*, dated Sunday, 17th April 2016, is the only newspaper clipping from my years in the public eye that I've kept. I've framed it and it hangs on my sitting room wall. For me, it represents the one instance I was in control and represented in the media fairly and neutrally, without flattery or denigration.

Two immediate and significant things happened in reaction to the *Observer* article. One: the police came to visit me and apologised. They said they would look into what had gone wrong. They didn't. Instead, they wrote me a letter blaming me for potentially preventing other victims seeking police help.

'*Dear Mrs Cooper,*' the letter reads. '*I have left you a voice mail to call me at your convenience. Please, as you know there have been press reports suggesting you are dissatisfied with the response you received. Further, due to the high profile of this matter, I fear other victims of similar crimes may have read the story, and now may not have the confidence in us to report such matters. As such it is really important that I can understand, what, if anything, went wrong during the investigation. I was saddened to hear of this report so would like to hear your views on what we could do better.*'

The second thing was a direct message via Twitter from the

journalist, Kirsty Wark. 'I've read the article in the *Observer*,' she wrote, 'and I want to do something on it. Is it OK if my producer calls you?'

I spoke to Ian Katz, the producer of *Newsnight*, at length. He was more measured than Catherine and Tracy and the women at Paladin. He wanted to find any holes in the story but, over the years, my assistant Vicky and I had logged everything. Apart from the letters we'd given to the police and which they'd destroyed, we'd carefully documented every alarming tweet and Instagram message from Alex Gray, as well as the various police reports we'd made over the years. I could tell him how many times my lawyer or my assistant had called or emailed the officers in charge of my case, asking for help or a progress report, and repeatedly been ignored. I could reassure Ian Katz that I wasn't overdramatising anything. I didn't want to moan about Alex Gray. I didn't want to go on and on about myself. I wanted to talk about the situation and the police's reaction to it. I thought: *If a white girl with two kids, living in a wealthy, Conservative* (at that time) *constituency, with a load of money to chuck at lawyers, can be mistreated like this, imagine what else is going on.*

If this had happened to me, then what was happening to the abused, vulnerable girls out there with no money and no lawyers and no private bodyguards? Does that other girl even exist in the system? Does she ever come forward? Is her voice heard? How often? How loudly? That's what I'm more interested in. If I feel short-changed and I've got it all, then how fucking short-changed must every other victim feel, and why isn't anything being done about it?

Once I'd gone through the story forensically with Ian, I had dinner with Kirsty Wark and we talked about it all some more. She'd read all the information I'd given Tracy and Ian, and we FaceTimed about it that night. The next day, in a little function room at the Charlotte Street Hotel in London, we filmed the interview, a section of which was on *Newsnight* the next night, with the longer version available to watch on the BBC website.

From that moment on I began to feel like I could sense closure. A year later, as I write this, I'm only really beginning to *feel* proper closure, but back then I did at last think, *The information is out there correctly; the wheels are back on; I didn't make it all up, or go mad.*

And I thought about who it was who had helped me, who it was who had listened to me and made things go right, who told the truth and acted responsibly: it was the women in my life, or who I had met.

It was my mum, Alison. It was Catherine Meyer. It was the women from Paladin. It was Tracy McVeigh. It was Kirsty Wark. As my marriage ended, and as a group of women helped me to grapple with one of the most traumatic and jarring experiences of my life, I began to realise that I could survive and eventually perhaps thrive on my own. That perhaps it was time to tackle that great, big, raging addiction that so often goes unchecked because it doesn't make you slur your words or shout too loudly or your liver pack up or your heart stop – at least not biologically.

I'm talking about co-dependency.

It was time, I realised, to begin to live my life as a mother and a writer and a singer, on my own terms.

BREAKDOWN

If only it were so easy.

Deciding to change a pattern of behaviour is commendable: *Great! Go girl!* Realising you're a dysfunctioning human being is honest and requires self-awareness and insight, and it's courageous to face up to that dysfunction. But real change doesn't happen overnight. Fuck, it takes work. I mean, I grew up witnessing my mum and my sister in their own co-dependent relationship, and that's what I yearned for. It also became my template for what I imagined a loving relationship to look like. I wanted to share the same kind of magic circle that I believed they were in. I was done with feeling alone, and as soon as I met Lester, that's what I did. I made our relationship so important that I felt like my life depended on it.

I repeated that pattern of needing someone around me all the time over and over again. If I was between boyfriends,

I made sure I attached myself firmly to Jess or Miquita or, if they were absent, one of my assistants. If I was seeing someone – even if it was a fling – I convinced myself that it was the beginning of a big thing. I ran into motherhood and marriage with Sam without taking enough time to build our relationship into something that might survive the challenges any couple inevitably faces. And I had done it using rocky foundations: if I was the cornerstone in our family life, no wonder the little edifice we made together became unstuck. I wasn't stable to begin with, and my career as a pop artist led to me feeling profoundly splintered as a person. That meant I wasn't able to cope well in the storms that rained down, as they do.

When George died, I responded first by drinking and then by getting pregnant as quickly as possible. When I felt like my first daughter, Ethel, was rejecting me, I didn't seek proper help for what was probably postnatal depression, but instead had another baby. After Marnie was born, I should have hunkered down and dealt with the issues facing me: financial demands, postnatal depression, and figuring out how better to combine my work with motherhood. Instead, I went on the road ostensibly to solve one of the problems and get money flowing back into our ecosystem – but ignored the others. They got worse.

I reached crisis point. I had to admit defeat and end my marriage, which meant facing up to the fact that I had failed to form a life partnership, failed to build the magic circle, failed to be dependable as a wife and failed at depending on Sam for all my needs. So it goes. It was time to begin from the bottom up, starting with letting Sam go properly and, with him, the identity I'd constructed as Mrs Cooper. It's hard to let go, though, of something like that – the person you'd desired to be, tried hard to create, and built a whole home around – without some shrapnel flying off.

★ ★ ★

A year later, quite a lot of shrapnel flew off. I didn't just lose my shit, like I had on the Marrakech shoot, I lost my mind. I exploded.

It had been a long time coming. Soon after making the decision to sell Overtown, in the winter of 2016, I went there for the weekend with the girls. I felt sad that this would be one of the last times we'd be at this home together, the place they loved, and I felt unhappy that the reason for this was because Sam and I hadn't made our marriage work. We couldn't afford to keep Overtown and having to sell it signified just how much we'd failed to keep our family together, as we'd once planned.

The car journey back to London that Sunday evening took a long time. I was tired and weary. I had a headache. The traffic was terrible. When we finally got back, I made the girls supper and settled them into bed. Then I prepared their packed lunches for their next day at school and nursery, and began half-heartedly making myself something to eat. It's lonely, doing that Sunday night thing all on your own.

The headache I'd had while driving got worse, and began to feel excruciating. The pain got so bad I began to worry. I called Sam. At this point we were making our best stab at being friends and because we were still locked into the vestiges of our co-dependency, we were not just friends but *best* friends. We talked ten times a day. We went to couples therapy. We shared looking after the kids fifty-fifty. We helped each other out with pick-ups and drop-offs. We had breakfast together once a week with the girls before school. All of this was positive, but it also signalled how difficult we both found it to let each other go off into the future without keeping tabs. You can decide to call it quits on a marriage over dinner, but unknitting a life you've made with someone is harder. It takes time, and to do it with grace takes a great deal of courage and generosity. We didn't always manage that.

I could tell on the phone that Sam was with someone when I called, and I could tell it was a girl. He came over to make sure I was OK, but he was distant. He clearly couldn't wait to get away. I realised I'd interrupted his evening.

I asked him about it the next morning. 'Look,' I said, 'you're obviously seeing someone, and that's good, but it's weird that you haven't told me.' As part of our separation therapy, Sam had insisted that I write down every detail of my infidelities. It had felt humiliating doing that, but Sam had been adamant about needing to know, and so I'd done it. I'd also told him when I'd got together with Dan, and exactly who Dan was, even though their paths didn't ever cross.

I felt like we'd agreed to be as open as possible about our lives and now he was keeping this big thing from me. 'It's not your business,' he kept saying. 'It's no big deal. Why do you need to know?'

'Because,' I said, 'not knowing is doing my head in.' Finally he told me. It did my head in more.

Sam was seeing a girl called Georgie. Georgie is a gorgeous-looking socialite with insanely long legs and blonde hair. Frankly, I would have preferred it if he'd started dating someone shorter and dumpier than me, but what can you do? What I found hard was that she appeared to be friends with lots of people from my life. I could see from Instagram that she'd been on a road trip across America with the girl Lester went out with immediately after chucking me. There they were, posing together in bikinis in Arizona. Another, more recent photograph, showed her hanging out with my assistant. And she'd been out at the pub with Mark Ronson, who I was working with in the studio right then. She'd had drinks with other friends, too. They'd all been back at each other's houses, hanging out.

It felt like she and Sam as a couple were *this* close to me, but just out of my vision. I felt like there was me in one corner, always dealing with everyone talking *about* the intimate details of my life, but with no one actually telling me anything that might be relevant or helpful *to* my life. I felt like no one was even trying to come into my corner. I found this upsetting. It felt like, *Fuck, this is how lonely I am now*. And yet, no one had betrayed me. No one had done anything wrong. Everyone was going about their business. It's just that I was outside it all. I couldn't even justify feeling angry. At least, that's what I told myself.

Sometimes, I let paranoia creep in, like I was surrounded by a web of secrets. I felt like Sam had an agenda and that he wasn't telling me about his relationship because we'd soon be selling Overtown, and it suited him for me to be the bad guy and for him to be the one who was left alone and hard done by. Either way, I felt isolated and like an outcast from my own life. Those may not have been valid feelings, but I felt them. After all, they are the feelings I am most familiar with and I find it easy to return and sometimes wallow in them. It's maddening, I know.

I spent the week in a haze of sadness and despair. The girls were with Sam for the week, and by Friday I had reached an awful place. I felt desolate. I took a lot of sleeping pills and slept for a long time. I remember waking up and thinking: *I don't want to wake up*, and so I took more pills. Poor Dan. He was with me through all this – not that I let him help me. It can't be easy to watch someone you love fall apart over her ex-husband. But Dan's not a narcissist. He didn't make it about him. He just tried to help me, and he didn't leave.

On Sunday night, I woke up, apparently. I don't remember any of it. I was on automatic, as if my body had been taken over by someone else. According to Dan, I jumped out of bed, grabbed my car keys and told him I was going to drive off a bridge. He tried to stop me leaving, but I was determined.

I didn't drive to a bridge. I went to Sam's house. By then, Dan had called Alfie and my mum in a panic. Mum knew I'd be at Sam's.

'Yes,' Sam said, when she called him. 'She's here. But you need to come and get her. She's behaving like a psycho.' I was screaming, apparently, pulling curtains down, smashing anything I could and kicking the walls.

BREAKDOWN

What upsets me most about my breakdown is that the girls saw me there at Sam's house. They saw me going mad. I spent a lot of my childhood watching my mum cry, and of course it's fine for children to see their parents crying – sometimes. But it's not their role to be comforters. I don't want my kids to think back to when they were little and associate it with their mum being sad. That's not how life should be. Life is precious and beautiful and it should be celebrated. Who am I kidding, right? But still. It is. We all know that, even when we fail at it. I want at least to try and deliver that message to my children even if I can't always, even if I can't often spread the good word through my own being. But that night my daughters saw their mum going mental. They were scared. I wish I could change that. I wish that hadn't happened.

Mum and Aaron, my mum's partner, came and picked me up from Sam's house and drove me home. I slept. Mum stayed the night.

The next morning I woke up and started up again. Fucking hell, I've got energy when I'm mad. I'm a determined bitch, I'll give myself that. I started on more self-harming, more smashing glass, more screaming and kicking and shouting. Poor Mum. She called my godmother, Henrietta, who lives nearby, and she came straight over. I greeted her by putting a cigarette out on my hand, then slamming my head repeatedly in a cupboard door.

'Alison,' Henrietta said, matter of factly, 'we need to call the doctor. She's gone.'

And I was gone. For all my endless resolutions to get better and get sane and get straight and stand alone and be well and stay healthy, in November 2016, I was gone. I was admitted to hospital.

I didn't use drugs any more and I hadn't since getting clean after the *Sheezus* tour, but when I was checked into the Nightingale clinic after my breakdown at Sam's, I was put on medication. I didn't want to take meds, but there are consequences if you have a psychotic episode.

The hospital didn't have to listen to my mum describe my behaviour, because I lost it there, too, when they told me I couldn't leave. I didn't want to take the pills they were giving me, but they told me I had no choice. 'You take these pills,' they said, 'or we'll section you.'

'I'm a voluntary patient,' I screamed at them. 'You can't section me.'

'We can,' they replied, 'and we will, unless you take these pills. And just so you know, your life will change once you've been sectioned. You'll be denied certain travel visas and, more importantly, you'll have social services coming to check on you and your children regularly until they're eighteen.'

They laid it out. I was livid. But the psychotic outbursts had come directly out of the anger I'd kept repressed inside me for so long. Finding out that Sam was seeing someone else was the first time I felt anger about everything that had happened in our marriage and separation, and it wasn't simply about Sam being in a new relationship. I felt angry with Sam, period. I had carried so much guilt and felt so much shame about what I'd done for so long. Now, all I could think was: *Hang on a minute. You took a vow to love and protect me, and you failed at that. You sent me off on tour in a traumatic state. You claimed responsibility for saving me when we first got together, so you knew exactly the environment I was going into, alone, without my children and without support, and yet you waved me off.*

Of course, in reality, we were both to blame for what happened. But my anger, destructive as it was, marked a new beginning. It was real. I'd shed my carapace. It was *me* shouting and screaming and kicking and railing. What came out of my breakdown was the beginning of feeling empowered. I had always taken responsibility for what had happened between me and Sam, but now, for the first time, I began to think: *It's not all my fault. I don't have to stay in the punishment corner by myself, cowering and apologising. I can get up and move on.*

I started to recover. I took the anti-psychotic pills, even though I didn't want to. Sometimes you have to do what you are told.

After two months I stopped taking them, winding down slowly as advised. I didn't miss them. I don't miss hard drugs now that I no longer take them. I drink, but not to excess. I don't miss getting out of it.

I was driving to a friend's house on a Saturday morning recently, when I saw a couple in their early twenties walking up Ladbroke Grove arm-in-arm, still wearing their Friday night glad-rags. They clearly hadn't been to bed. I watched them while I waited at a set of traffic lights, and my whole body felt heavy. I could imagine exactly what they'd been doing all night long, the chats they'd been having, the drugs they'd been taking, and the way they were feeling that morning. *Enjoy it, guys*, I thought. *Enjoy that walk and that high.*

Then I looked behind me at my two children strapped into

their car seats, chatting away to each other, and I thought, *This is where I should be.*

FORWARDS

About a month before my breakdown, I went to Calais. You may have seen the television footage of me there, talking to a young teenager from Afghanistan. It seems everybody did. I broke down in tears talking to him and then apologised 'on behalf of my country' because it seemed clear to me that when it came to the Jungle, we were all complicit in a dereliction of duty. I went there not to become a news story myself, but because a friend of mine called Josie had started working for the charity Help Refugees, and she wanted to highlight the issue of unaccompanied child refugees being denied a safe passage to the UK.

I couldn't say no when she invited me to see for myself what it was like – nor did I want to. I've always felt strongly about the benefits of living in an inclusive society, and as a Londoner I experience them every single day. I've had the privilege of growing up around people from all over the world. *Of course* we should be welcoming child refugees into our country. As if we could do anything else. You don't turn children away. It's unthinkable. But to talk about it more, I wanted to be more informed. I wanted to see the Jungle for myself.

It was a huge shantytown. People were friendly to us, but you could see how easily things might become dangerous. You could see many young people having to survive alone. I worried for the girls especially. That's when I apologised, in tears, to the young Afghani boy. I wish I hadn't. It wasn't appropriate, and I wish I'd done a better job of keeping myself together. That's when I apologised to him 'on behalf of my country' too. It was a clumsy thing to say. I wanted to say, 'I'm sorry,' and I wanted to acknowledge that I was part of the problem, and that we are all part of the problem if we don't do more to help. The words came out badly, and for that I felt foolish. I was embarrassed about putting it like that. I can be a moron. But my intentions were straightforward and without any agenda. I just wanted to help, in whatever tiny way I could.

I got a lot of stick about my visit to Calais. I've always been trolled and bullied on social media, but after Calais the online bullying I experienced went off the charts. People jumped to conclusions and made assumptions about everything I said: when I said, for example, that I believed our invasion of Iraq was wrong, they accused me of slandering the Armed Forces as a whole. People wrote in violent terms about what they'd like to do to me and what I deserved. They often included my kids when they discussed dishing out my punishments. I minded all that.

★ ★ ★

I still mind, and the bullying still goes on, and sometimes I fight back. I know people say, *Oh, just ignore the tweets and the comments and the abuse and block the bullies and it'll go away,* and occasionally I do, but I also think: *No.* Ignoring bullies and letting them give voice to bigotry and threaten violence without rebuke or redress is a kind of silence I'm not interested in.

I don't react well to being bullied or backed into a corner. I don't want to be silent. That's why I keep tweeting – even though my Twitter feed is hijacked by people tweeting hateful comments. Often this takes the form of men consistently tweeting the same three charges against me to prove their point and win their argument. The charges are 1) I'm a bad mother; 2) I'm famous because of my dad; and 3) I'm stupid. In other words, what they do is belittle me. Because if you shout at someone enough and tell her she's a dumb woman who wouldn't be anywhere without her dad, then she'll shut up, right?

Example: I was tweeting about a Theresa May speech recently and someone tweeted: 'Oi, Lily, can I smell your privates?'

I replied: 'Yeah, sure, but you might want to wait because I'm on the blob.'

My Twitter feed went mad. People were outraged. 'How can you say that?' the tweets went. 'No wonder everyone hates you,' they went on, 'when you talk like that.'

I was, like, *What planet are we on? This guy just asked to sniff my privates but I mention my period and I'm the one who is disgusting?*

I don't think that the men who run the tabloids and who berate me on Twitter like women much. Not just women, either. I think they're scared of anyone who isn't like them, who isn't white and middle class and male. Because those men who run things, they aren't necessarily cleverer or better than everyone else, but for some reason they've managed to make all the rules for hundreds and hundreds of years. No wonder they're resentful and defensive when the rest of us are angry and have decided that we want a bit of what they've got. So it's like, 'NO. *You* can't have a piece. You're disgusting, you've got a vagina. No, *you*'re not having any of it, either, because you're black and you're a criminal. And *you*? You're Asian, you've probably got a bomb under there, so you're not allowed any of it, either. You're all threatening to me so I'm going to vilify and bully you as much as I can to silence and shame you.'

I don't want to be silent. Women have been silenced for millennia, and I'm not going to be part of that. I want to speak up, and if that means I sometimes get it wrong, then I should be able to correct myself, apologise, move on and *still* carry on speaking up. As a woman, I'm not meant to be an angel or a saint or a martyr or to have faultless encyclopaedic answers all the time. I'm a woman only, and, like all women, I don't ask for special treatment. Like all women, I just ask not to be repressed or silenced.

I've never been saintly. I know I'm a narcissist. I can behave badly. I'm capable of self-sabotage and self-destruction. I have a history of mental illness, drug abuse and addictive behaviour. I can be petulant and spoilt, short-tempered and stubborn.

But even when I'm deep in foggy, cloudy behaviour, numbing myself with whatever I can, some part of me remains self-aware. I'm hyper *hyper* self-aware. It's what has kept me from going under. I've sometimes felt like I've been drowning and lost and as if I've disappeared, but I've always stopped myself, even if it's in a destructive way with drugs, or hospitalisation, from losing it completely.

I think it's one of the reasons why I both perform and why, counterintuitively, I rarely lose myself in a performance. It's why I'll never be a world-class singer. I'm not talking about my voice range or my tonal abilities. Those aren't the things that are holding me back. I don't want to be a world-class singer. That was never my intention or desire. I'm not like Adele say, or Amy Winehouse, who both knew from an early age that using their vocals was their destiny.

But still, when people identify me, mostly they say: 'Lily Allen, pop star.' I was indeed a pop star. That's what I became, serving my apprenticeship in public for everyone to see. The problem is, like most people in their early twenties, I was also trying to figure out who the hell I was as a person, and doing that while inhabiting Popstardomland is especially tricky and confusing.

On the one hand, you're treated like a child: spoiled and indulged at every juncture. You check into a hotel and your room has been upgraded. There is a bottle of Cristal up there in an ice bucket waiting for you. *Of course we'll send a car for you. We'd love to send you a hamper of beauty products. Please wear this dress.*

Cue reactions of: *Wow, this is so great. I love all this. Lucky me.*

Which then leads to, as the spoiling becomes normalised: *Why is the car late? Why is there this shitty champagne and not ice-cold Cristal?* Which morphs into, when you're overtired, far away from home, lonely as fuck and feeling like you're dying inside: *What the fuck? I fucking hate Cristal, get it the fuck out of here. Fuck, fuck, fuck!*

But then, right at the very same time as all this molly-coddling, you've got to deal with all this other super-grown-up stuff that no one prepares you for. Signing scary contracts. Taking on accountants. Running up huge bills that you are hardly aware of. Hiring people. Firing them. I know that entering any career has its learning curves, its challenges and difficulties as well as its rewards, but the thing about pop stardom is that these things – the challenges and the rewards – are amplified to a huge degree and if you achieve success quickly, as I did, you don't get to practise any of it. It turns out there is no real apprenticeship programme for fame, which means you are ill-prepared to handle it and, as a result, you stumble. You stumble publicly.

The tabloids love it when you do that. Their cartoon version of you becomes writ so large that people start to believe it. At times, you begin to believe it yourself.

People think you're a cartoon, they write about you as if you're a cartoon, and they treat you like you're a cartoon, and so, yes, you start to think of yourself as a cartoon and behave like one, too, and the vicious circle perpetuates itself.

Everything changed when I lost George. That's when I thought: *Oh my God, I'm a person, a real person, not a cartoon one blundering through a life where nothing matters too much.* (Thanks, Dad.) *In fact, I've got these emotions and feelings and I don't know where to put them or what to do with them and I can't pretend any longer that they don't exist or don't matter.* That was when I started learning how to become a more functioning human being. That's taken an apprenticeship, too.

It turns out I'm not a pop star, per se. That was part of a ripple effect of what I do, and perhaps it will be again. It was a stage along the way: an odd Alice-in-Wonderland, exciting, tricky, confusing chapter. It turns out I'm a songwriter. It turns out my job is to write about what I see and what I've learned and what I feel and what I know. I then sing out those words using the best voice I can. It's not world-class, but it's honest and it's true.

I want, even if it's just for my daughters, for it to be strong and loud and clear.

NOW

nearly called my latest album *The Fourth Wall*. The title made sense to me because I rarely lose myself on stage or in my performances. I'm always aware of the audience and never behind the fourth wall. Plus, the record is my fourth album, and I like wordplay so the title worked on lots of levels. It was both an invitation: 'Come into my world,' and an explanation about my new work: 'Yes, I'm a performer and these are songs, but none of it is *really* a performance. It's just me. My words are true. This is how I feel, this is what I've been through, this is how I see things.'

Then I thought, *If the whole point of this record is my honesty, why am I going for wordplay? Why not get straight to the point? Who cares about conceptual levels of meaning?* I thought, *I need to simply say what I mean and feel.*

And that's why I called the album *No Shame*.

When Seb – who knows me better than anyone else – and I

started working together on this record, he said to me, 'What do you want, Lily? Do you want fame and money, or do you want to make a record that is real and honest?'

'The latter,' I replied.

'Good,' said Seb. 'As long as we stick to that, let's do it.'

That's what we've done. We've made the record we want to make, without compromising the songs. I still don't get to call all the shots, because I don't write all the cheques. I will have to listen to what the label wants too, and no doubt I'll have to make compromises when it comes to marketing my work. But I haven't been scared to say no this time round. And if I feel like I have to drink a couple of glasses of champagne to get dressed or pose or behave in a certain way, then I'll know: *This isn't right. This isn't me. This isn't working.* And I'll say no. I'm not doing sexy-face again.

I'm a performer, yes, but I'm also a mother and a daughter and a sister and a partner and an ex-wife and a friend and a writer and a collaborator, and I've finally learned that not one of these roles need be repressed in service to the others. Of course we all compartmentalise ourselves to a degree. We have to. None of us can be everything to everyone all the time. When I'm at work, the mother in me must accept that she needs to wait her turn. When I'm writing, I have to banish the friend who would welcome distraction. When I'm with my children, my other roles must wait in line. But none of them needs be dismissed. I'm still a mother when I perform and write, still a writer and singer when I'm with my children. I realise now that I don't have to pretend or fake things or divide myself into multiple parts. I can, instead, remain whole. We should all be able to live and work on our own terms, with integrity and without shame. I haven't always done it, but people do, and that's what I'm after. That's what I'm striving for.

I've begun by reclaiming my voice. I felt stunned into silence when that first tabloid headline appeared on the front cover of *The News of the World*, just as 'Smile' went to number one. From that moment on, I still spoke out, but I felt fearful. Whatever I said could be twisted or turned or blown up big or taken out of context. It was like I had this invisible, nebulous, all-knowing, all-watching censorious gas that wafted around me all the time. That's one reason why drink and drugs felt safe: they allowed me to blot out the fear, at least to an extent. *You can't express opinions*, the fear said. *Get back in your fucking box*, it said. *We'll decide who you are, and we'll tell the world about it and one day we might decide that you're unworthy and disgusting and the next we might decide that you're great. You don't get to decide that. We do.*

Not any more, motherfuckers! I don't feel fear any more. The worst already happened, and it had nothing to do with anything I said or did. I lost my child, and it was just one of those things.

I want my voice back.
I'm getting my voice back.
Here I am.
Listen.
I've got my voice back.

ACKNOWLEDGEMENTS

Claire, my agent, for asking me to do this in the first place. Everyone at Blink, but especially Beth, who has the patience of a saint. Seb, Sarah, my wonderful boyfriend Dan and my children for putting up with me. My secret helper who shall go unnamed and my silent partner who helps me make sense of things.

Me, Mum & Dad, 1985

Feeding Time

Dressing Up

Me & Mum

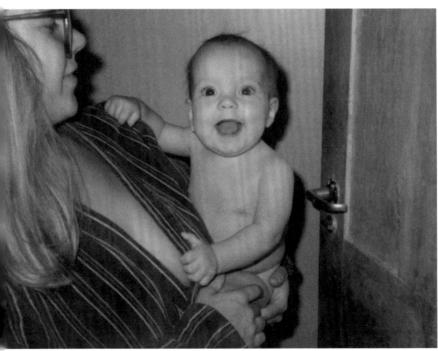

Number One

Me & Dad

Alfie, Mum & Dad on set in Spain for a UB40 Music Video

Bath Time

Two

Ice Cream

Three

Says It All

Mum, Paul Cantelon & Me in Ireland

Dad, Alfie & Me

Me & Alfie, Bloomsbury

Five

Ingersoll Road, Shepherd's Bush, with dog Lucy

Summer Holiday

Feeding Time

Me, Alfie, Mum & Wasp. Ottawa, Canada

Snape Maltings, Suffolk

Lady in Waiting E

Ladies in Waiting A, B, C, D, E and Cate Blanchett as Elizabeth

**Planet Hollywood,
9th Birthday**

Sunday Best

Me & Sarah, Majorca

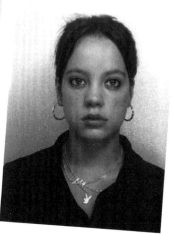

**Awkward Teenager
Continued**

I Love You